"Each of us wants to *thrive* in our career and, more importantly, our personal life. David McNally provides a framework to define what that truly means and a wonderful road map to getting there."
— Roger J. Dow, Vice President and
   General Sales Manager, Marriott

"David McNally has provided a highly thought-provoking approach on how to thrive in both our personal and professional lives."
— James McGuirk, II, President,
   Unysis Corporation

"*The Eagle's Secret* has had a huge impact on my career in professional sports. This is a mandatory read for anyone who wants to soar with the eagles."
— Pat Williams, executive senior vice president, Orlando Magic

"If you consider learning to be a lifelong process, then you will be flooded with new insights as David McNally takes you on a masterfully engineered journey of self-discovery."
— Tim Foley, Crown Ambassador Distributors, Amway Corporation

"David McNally's inspirational, proactive approach to business and life strategies permeates each chapter of *The Eagle's Secret*. McNally is a Master Communicator."
— Rick Tippett, director, national advertising, *The Washington Post*

"*The Eagle's Secret* is a refreshing combination of tools, quotes, and intellectual challenges that will elevate you personally and professionally."
— Klaus-Dieter Schuermann, CEO,
   Volkswagen Credit/Audi Financial Services

"David McNally's book is one I want my children, my wife, and all my employees to read. It will profoundly affect their lives."
— Leo Taylor, vice president,
   Human Resources, Pulte Home Corporation

"David McNally made a real impact while speaking at a conference for our top performers. *The Eagle's Secret* has even broader appeal because companies need thrivers."
— Burvin Pugh, senior vice president,
   Massachusetts Mutual Life Insurance Co.

"I found *The Eagle's Secret* relates to the real world and not some theoretical situation. It was enlightening, entertaining and motivated me to make some very important personal changes."
—Alan Westwood, leader, Hewlett-Packard,
Global Project Management Initiative

"David McNally challenges us to continue to learn about ourselves so that we can thrive. *The Eagle's Secret* provides not only important insights but also the steps on how to do it."
—Greg Schatzlein, director of training, Ameritech

"Leadership is about building and sustaining relationships. *The Eagle's Secret* gives us the courage to look at ourselves honestly so that we can thrive rather than just survive."
—Dr. Roger Sublett, director, Kellogg National Leadership Program

"I keep *The Eagle's Secret* on my desk because I refer to it so often. David McNally has done a superb job weaving stories, exercises, and quotes into an inspiring text."
—Ron Campbell, president, Center for Leadership Studies

David McNally

The Eagle's Secret

Success Strategies for Thriving at Work & in Life

A Dell Trade Paperback

A DELL TRADE PAPERBACK

Published by
Dell Publishing
a division of
Random House, Inc.
1540 Broadway
New York, New York 10036

ISBN: 0-440-50845-2

For information on how to contact David McNally, call 1-800-228-1218 or visit his Web site at www.foreverlearning.com.

Reprinted by arrangement with Delacorte Press
Printed in the United States of America
Published simultaneously in Canada

May 1999

10   9   8   7   6   5   4   3   2

RRD

TO MY DAD

THE VERY BEST OF ROLE MODELS

and

TO MY WIFE

THE VERY BEST OF PARTNERS

ACKNOWLEDGMENTS

I thought that writing a second book might be somewhat easier than the first. It was not. In my world, however, I am privileged to know many generous souls. This work made it to publication because they would not allow me to give up. To all of you who read what I wrote and responded with ideas, comments, and encouragement, my only hope is that you feel your time was well invested.

Assisting me with the early research were some of the best writers in the business, Scott Edelstein, Peter Kizilos, Susan Reed, Betty McMahon, and Ron Lehmann. They were committed collaborators and their expertise and influence are reflected throughout the pages. Jonathon Lazear, my agent, listened with sensitivity to my frustrations, and Tom Spain, my editor, exercised considerable patience as he coaxed me into what I now see as very important enhancements.

My desire to be different was once again realized through the creativity of Lisa Etziony. Lisa designed the cover and the pages with the sole purpose of making the printed word inviting and accessible. Her talent and dedication shines through.

Jo McNally, my wife, is that special friend who knows all about me but loves me just the same. Jo Reinhart is my office manager and to her I am most grateful for being so loyal, competent, and completely dependable.

Finally, there are my family and friends, whose presence makes me feel I matter. We enjoy many good times together, but it is when life is not so good that you always seem to be there. Thank you.

PREFACE - PAGE IX

CHAPTER 1 - PAGE 1
The Economic Earthquake
A Whole Lotta Shakin' Goin' On

CHAPTER 2 - PAGE 33
The Principle of Contribution
How The World Works

CHAPTER 3 - PAGE 55
Personal Responsibility
It's 6:00 AM and You're Still In Bed?

CHAPTER 4 - PAGE 77
Forever Learning
When You're Green You Grow, When You're Ripe You Rot

CHAPTER 5 - PAGE 105
Discovering Your Genius
A Star Is Born

CHAPTER 6 - PAGE 143
A Question of Trust
She's Your Brother

CHAPTER 7 - PAGE 183
Nourishing Heart, Mind & Soul
Three-Part Harmony

CHAPTER 8 - PAGE 209
What's It All About?
From Success to Significance

Preface

Nothing happens without transformation.

W. EDWARDS DEMING

To the reader from the author — These words are being written as I am coaching and coaxing a sixteen-year-old daughter through what she regards as the "worst" period of her life. Her friends have deserted her, she has put on weight, the braces on her teeth are killing her, but, more important, no guy, especially the ones she's attracted to, will give her a second glance.

I remember my own teenage years only too well to dismiss her pain as unimportant. Her tears are real, for pain is pain, no matter the cause, and although I believe she will come through with flying colors, I also know that her strength and resilience as an adult is built from knowing she can handle these early passages in her life.

I was struck by the correlation between the counsel to my daughter and the work we shall be doing together throughout the following pages. *The Eagle's Secret* is about thriving, it's about growing and flourishing, it's about taking charge of our lives and turning our dreams into reality. My daughter may be barely "surviving" this summer, but her essence, who she is as a human being, could not be described in any other way than that of a "thriver."

To survive means to continue to exist, to not die. If you are alive you are a survivor. There are times when surviving requires a supreme effort. We witness the heroism of people all over the world in their struggle just to exist. But their drive to survive, they will tell you, is in large part inspired by their desire to thrive. To thrive means to grow and prosper.

You and I are living in fascinating times. Opportunities are abundant no matter whether you're called to the world of business, to save the planet, or to be involved in some other worthy cause. More people have more freedom to enjoy peace and prosperity than at any time in history. Now, of course, not everybody sees it that way. An employee of one large company described many people's feelings when she reported: "Everybody's under pressure. Some are being healthy, they're exercising and running. Some people are just eating more chocolate." In other words, for some it is the best of times, for others, the worst.

For those eating the chocolate, it seems the endless corporate restructuring, compelled by an ever more competitive global economy, has produced a sense of instability and loss of control that is adversely affecting their lives and their futures. Mere survival has become their highest hope and aspiration. While this reaction is understandable, who are those other people who are exercising and running? Why, under the same conditions and circumstances, do they appear to be thriving?

The desire to thrive means the desire to live a life rich in experiences and accomplishment. Somerset Maugham said: "It's a funny thing about life, if you refuse to accept anything but the best you very often get it." Thrivers agree, and so they think and act in ways that lead them to the very best that life has to offer. What is so clearly observable and distinguishes thrivers, therefore, is their attitudes and behaviors. While the survivors struggle for a sense of direction, thrivers navigate steadily and relentlessly toward their goals.

While survivors get tossed about by the turbulence of modern existence, thrivers soar to new heights of personal achievement.

If your desire is to be a thriver, the following question is an excellent starting point: How much time do you allocate each week to sitting back and reflecting on what you do, why you do it, what's important to you, and in what direction your life is heading? When giving a workshop or a speech, I often pose this question to my audience. More often than not, the response is an amazing silence. It seems that in the busyness of our lives, we rarely take the time to think about the business of life. Often we are very clear about what the company wants, but we are not so sure of what we want. That will not work for those committed to thriving.

In the pages that follow, you will be getting to the "bottom line" of what you truly want for your life and how to achieve it. You will clarify what thriving looks like to you, how thriving feels, and what being a thriver will mean to the quality of your life. Not only will you map out where you want to go, you also will be able to check daily if you're on the right path. You are about to embark on quite an adventure, in every sense of the word.

Many of the ideas, insights, and stories about thriving revealed in this book came from a survey sent to over six hundred people. Their roles and responsibilities covered a large section of for-profit and not-for-profit organizations. From the wonderful response, it was evident that I had clearly touched a nerve. CEO's to first-line supervisors responded, as did educators, salespeople, and entrepreneurs. I asked for examples of people who were thriving in their organizations and for them to explain why, in terms of specific attitudes and behaviors. They shared their experiences most generously, for which I am deeply grateful.

What was striking about all responders was their enthusiasm and the value they perceived in identifying the characteristics of the thriver. Quite a few took the time to share personal stories about thriving, many of which are retold in the book. They range from the poignant and inspiring to specific how tos. What is most important to our work, however, is the powerful themes that emerged about what it takes to thrive. These themes provided the titles and inspired the content of each chapter.

I must confess, however, to having harbored a hidden agenda: Would a "secret" be revealed? Would this secret finally explain why some people thrived while others just survived? Let me state right now that any notion I had that thrivers might be intellectually or physically superior had to be discarded quickly. Thrivers also were not blessed with excessive luck, although good fortune was certainly a frequent visitor to them, they did not escape much of life's pain and setbacks.

Eventually I learned, however, that thrivers do have a secret. It is a secret because it cannot be described, it has to be discovered. Are you ready to make that discovery? If so, then let's begin our journey.

DAVID MCNALLY
JUNE 1998

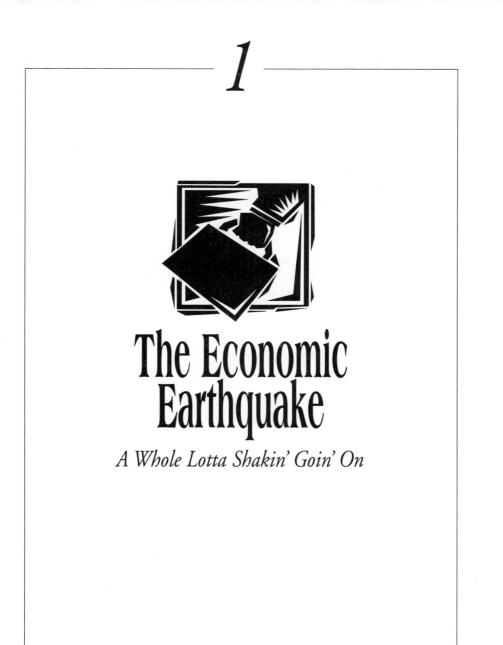

The Economic Earthquake

A Whole Lotta Shakin' Goin' On

Thrivers have a global perspective —
they are aware that major forces are transforming the world of work.

A MAN WAS CALLED FOR JURY DUTY and it looked like he might be chosen for a case that would drag on for some time. He asked the judge to excuse him. "We're very busy at the office," he exclaimed. "I can't afford to stay away for an extended period."

"I see," said the judge. "You're one of those people who feel that their organization just can't function without them. Is that right?"

"Oh, no, your Honor. I know they can get along without me. I just don't want them to find out."

If humor reflects the undercurrents of society, many of us readily identify with this story. A friend of mine said: "I hear you're writing a book about thriving. Well, I hope it's not full of that carpe diem, seize the day stuff. Let me tell you, by the time I get home from work and get the kids to bed, I'm lucky to have survived the day."

Reactions like those of my friend could have come from any one of thousands of people. Stress and exhaustion are among the most popular ailments of our time. Fear and anxiety are more prevalent than ever. Cynicism is fashionable. But, surely, this is not what you and I want. Are there other options, however? Is it possible to experience a sense of stability and control over our lives when most of what surrounds us is so clearly beyond our control?

For answers, the search always must begin inwardly, for the circumstances of our lives have as much power as we choose to give them. We need to discover if there is within us a sense of hope or, at least, a speck of faith that life has greater possibilities. For it is faith and hope that spark the strength and energy to persist, to push on toward a better life. For Vaclav Havel, the Czechoslovakian poet and playwright, the stresses and strains of feeling out of control were a persistent part of his daily life. Havel was imprisoned for his stand against communism, yet he emerged victorious to become the first president of his liberated country. "Life is too precious," Havel stated, "to permit its devaluation by living pointlessly, emptily, without meaning, without love, and, finally, without hope."

If faith and hope exist, even if just faintly flickering, our vision of thriving is attainable.

Charting our course, however, will require a different map, a new and greatly expanded perspective of how we see the world and our place in it. We must make a significant leap in our consciousness and knowledge, for ignorance is a major contributor to feelings of being powerless over our circumstances.

We must know much more about the world's economic systems and ecological systems. We need a greater understanding of other nations and their people, how they think, what they value. We must develop new skills and competencies, for our value to those whom we serve is coming under ever

The circumstances of our lives have as much power
as we choose to give them.

David McNally

The
Eagle's
Secret

greater scrutiny. Above all, we need to know much more about ourselves and the inherent power we have to create what we want for our lives.

In other words, if life is to be more than mere existence, if we are to move from survivor to thriver, it will not be through chance or good luck, it will be because we purposefully sought to understand and learn about what, with ever increasing momentum, is transforming the world around us.

But where should we begin?

Perhaps the most relevant place might be the most pragmatic, the issues and circumstances that affect our financial well-being. How will I pay my bills? What is the future of my career, my company, my industry, my country? These are questions that deserve answers. And, even if those answers are not ideally what we would like to hear, if they provide an honest assessment of where we stand, we can determine the actions we need to take to move in the direction we wish to go.

Here then is where we are today and where we undoubtedly will be for a considerable time into the future. A new world order is developing. Boundaries, borders, and businesses are on the move making fundamental shifts from which there is no turning back. These shifts are causing an economic earthquake of global proportions. "The world's landscape is unobstructed," said John Van Doorn in a recent *World Business* magazine editorial, "the view is, if imperfect, excellent. No wall, no river, no bureaucracy, no chauvinistic principles, can block it."

Understanding the forces contributing to this economic earthquake is a vital first step in learning how we might best respond and benefit from them. The most dominant forces are:

■ **TECHNOLOGY** — now expanding at warp speed. This is pushing us all back to school with no graduation date in sight.

■ **INTERNATIONAL COMPETITION** — on an unprecedented scale. This is demanding we produce an ever higher quality in both products and services.

■ **COMMUNICATIONS** — which have created a global village. What is happening, as it happens, in the lives and cultures of those who cohabit our planet is available twenty-four hours a day in our living rooms.

The implication of these forces is significant. In brief, the world is more open and transparent. More specifically, values, beliefs, assumptions, attitudes, and prejudices are all more visible, more exposed, and more subject to question and challenge. It is becoming increasingly difficult to avoid or "hide" from one's responsibilities. Politicians are being held accountable for their actions. Businesses are being put under a microscope. Individual contributions are being measured by more and more organizations.

In his book *The 12 New Rules for Living*, Frederic M. Hudson says: "Global change is the major reality for everyone on earth today. Rule: Don't whine! Pursue the benefits of chaos. They outnumber the problems." As our

When reality confronts our notion of what
reality should be, reality always wins.

John Roger and Peter McWilliams

The
Eagle's
Secret

desire is to thrive not whine, what else do we need to understand in order to boldly enter this turbulent, yet opportunity-filled, environment?

Just as there are more nations participating in the Olympic Games today than at any other time in history, more nations than ever are investing heavily in their infrastructures and economies so that their products and services can compete in the great game of business. A *BusinessWeek* editorial stated: "Billions of people are joining the world economy, not as beggars but as producers. A new economic order is being born. Eventually, the entire world should share the bounty of this new order."

The global economy is now such a reality and so advanced that there is clearly no turning back. We are, unquestionably, participating in an Olympics of Business. In other words, just as there are thousands of hungry young athletes itching to make the big time, so are there millions of people around the world with a burning desire to create the prosperity so prevalent and visible in the developed nations.

Now, while some would respond to that *BusinessWeek* prediction of abundance and prosperity with enthusiasm, many would prefer Woody Allen's idea of reassurance: "If God would only give me some clear sign! Like making a deposit in my Swiss bank account." Like me, however, if you have neither a Swiss bank account nor are inclined to make such requests of God, how might we best prepare ourselves to get our share of this coming bounty? First, by reemphasizing that any failure to deepen our understanding of the transformational forces now in play is a clear path to economic and career suicide.

During a recently televised conference for journalism students, the following statistic was discussed: Only 15 percent of the American public is interested in foreign news. What are the consequences of such a large group of people remaining ignorant of what is happening in the rest of the world?

Once more the Olympics provide a powerful analogy. Consider a coach or competitor from any nation who spends little, if any, time studying or learning about the competition. He or she has no idea of the strengths and weaknesses, speed, resilience, history, favorite strategies, attitudes, and size of the opponents. Can you now imagine how difficult it would be for this person to succeed? Today knowledge of the competition from high school to the pros is a key component of the formula for winning.

The proliferation of international trade agreements in every corner of the world provides undeniable evidence as to the course most nations have chosen. The Olympics of Business is definitely in play but with one important caveat: Unlike the Olympic Games, business does not have the luxury of four-year intervals to rest, recuperate, and prepare. In fact, new world records are being showcased everyday as competition raises the bar and customers raise their expectations.

To compete effectively organizations, large and small, are rapidly becoming more agile, creative, and responsive. Work is being redesigned radically with teams of people able and willing to anticipate, collaborate, negotiate, and innovate. And if that's not all, the commitment of each team member is being measured by the quality of his or her work.

An optimist thinks that this is the best of all worlds.
A pessimist fears that the same may be true.

Thomas A. Edison

The
Eagle's
Secret

To thrive in this transformed world, therefore, necessitates a level of personal development never before remotely considered by large sections of society. Millions are being forced out of narrow definitions of who they are, what they do, and what they can be. We all are being pushed to grow, to mature, and to soar. But even if we truly can grasp the urgency of this need for change and growth, how do we best prepare ourselves mentally and emotionally so that we are up to the challenge?

This is the journey that you and I are embarking upon. Wonderfully, we shall have plenty of support. As part of our team we shall have those people who thoughtfully responded to my survey and the real-life stories of the thrivers they wrote about. We also shall call upon the wisdom of the well known and not so well known in our world who, because of their own commitment to thriving, are a never-ending source of inspiration and information. During the journey we shall be taking an honest look at the increasing demands of the work world and developing strategies for reaching our professional and personal goals.

The accomplishment of any of these objectives will require, however, that you and I be clear about our roles and responsibilities. My primary role is to provide direction, yours is to choose the destination. I shall give guidance, you must make the decisions. I shall establish the questions, but you must discover the answers. In other words, where you want to go and how you want to get there, in the final analysis, can be determined only by you. As a caution, know that we are bound to hit some turbulence along the way. It will be an exciting ride, but there also may be some discomfort as you begin to move toward what you truly want in life. But I'm committed to this journey; are you? If so, then it's "all systems go!"

Very few people in today's work world have not been deeply involved in the process of restructuring and reengineering within their organizations. Reengineering as applied to business is defined as the fundamental rethinking and radical redesign of processes to bring about dramatic improvements in performance. Restructuring is the removal of organizational impediments to quick yet effective decision making. Although reengineering and restructuring have separate and distinct objectives, they share a common purpose: to create a more customer-focused, productive, and profitable enterprise.

When executed thoughtfully and properly, these processes have achieved their purpose. In many instances, however, these changes have not been painless, and have affected dramatically the lives of many people.

One employee, speaking to a friend, said: "The pressure is killing me. I have migraines, my cholesterol is going through the roof, I can't sleep at night, I just found out I have an ulcer, and as long as I stay in this job the only question is whether I have a stroke or a heart attack!" "So why don't you quit?" asked the friend. "I have a great health plan" came the reply.

Avoiding the heart attack or stroke lies, ironically, in learning from the processes that went into the restructuring and reengineering of our

The pessimist may be right in the long run,
but the optimist has a better time during the trip.

Anonymous

organizations, but this time applying them to our own professional and personal lives. We might call it personal **restructuring and reengineering**.

> *John Smith runs a large division of a building products company. He is not a college graduate and has not been computer literate. In a short period of time, information systems were beginning to play an important role in the marketing of his products. Rather than agonizing over the winds of change, he immediately upgraded his information services department with the best talent he could find. Then off to school he went, attending several intensive seminars (including one at Harvard) so that he could stay up to speed.*
>
> *This was not a one-shot burst of energy but a program of continuous self-improvement that has been going on for his entire twenty-three years with our company. His constant quest for improvement permeates his entire organization.*

> DONALD GOLDFUS – CHAIRMAN, APOGEE ENTERPRISES INC.

Personal restructuring and reengineering is the process of aligning what the world needs with what we are willing and able to contribute to it. The new world of work is demanding this level of introspection. In other words, we must be willing to reflect seriously on who we are and what we want our lives to be about. This will not be a mechanical, soulless exercise, however, as thriving, for us, means prospering in all areas of our lives. As we seek ways to improve our personal performance, simultaneously we will be focused on ensuring that our level of personal satisfaction increases as well. The ultimate vision is performance with fulfillment.

But where does this process begin?

In principle that question is simple to answer: The achievement of any vision must have as its starting point a no-nonsense assessment of current reality. What appears simple, however, is not always easy because, in this case, we must be ruthlessly honest with ourselves about how we currently think and feel about our lives. But, if we are truly committed to becoming thrivers, it is an exercise we must undertake. So sharpen your pencil and get ready to complete the Thriving Inventory.

The purpose of this inventory is to give you the opportunity to reflect on the attitudes and behaviors that play a significant role in your life. It is your thoughts and actions that shape your life and bring, or fail to bring, the results, in terms of personal and professional success, that you seek.

This inventory is not a test. It is meant, however, to be provocative and challenging so as to provide you with insight as to where you are positioned at this moment on your journey to becoming a thriver. As with any journey, it is wise to take stock not only of how you got to where you are but also what you still have to do to reach your destination.

The inventory contains forty-two pairs of attitudinal and behavioral descriptions. Each pair of statements represents the opposite ends of a six-point continuum. Be prepared to dislike some of the choices. It might appear that you are admitting to "weaknesses" or "unproductive tendencies." But do not label either choice "good" or "bad." View them as simply the way, at this moment, you look at or approach things. Doing this will allow you to be more candid and honest, resulting in a more useful and effective assessment.

THE THRIVING INVENTORY

DIRECTIONS: For each pair, circle a number on the scale that best represents your tendency as you see it. The extremes (1 and 6) represent very definite patterns of preferential attitudes and behavior, whereas the middle ratings (3 and 4) represent no particularly strong preference for either of the descriptions. It may be difficult to decide as you ponder the meaning of certain statements, but be sure to circle a number on the scale for each of the forty-two pairs. Avoid the middle ratings as much as possible.

1				
I get concerned that all this change is for the good	1 2 3 4 5 6			The more things change, the more I like it
2				
I cannot quite grasp how some people have so much money	1 2 3 4 5 6			I have learned that money is a reward for service
3				
I feel a little up in the air about what life has in store for me	1 2 3 4 5 6			I feel very relaxed about what life has in store for me
4				
I prefer to stay in my own corner of the world	1 2 3 4 5 6			I love to explore new horizons
5				
People can be so complex, I find that very challenging	1 2 3 4 5 6			People can be so complex; I find that very stimulating
6				
I identify most with the song "Stop the World, I Want to Get Off"	1 2 3 4 5 6			I identify most with the song "I Got a Lot of Living to Do"
7				
It is a long time since I have given serious thought to my goals	1 2 3 4 5 6			I am very clear about what I want to achieve

My reality is that "just keeping up" is a major accomplishment	**8** *1*	*2*	*3*	*4*	*5*	*6*	My reality is "staying ahead of the game" is essential
I believe I do a fair day's work for a fair day's pay	**9** *1*	*2*	*3*	*4*	*5*	*6*	I believe I provide value over and above my pay
If things are not perfect, I get frustrated	**10** *1*	*2*	*3*	*4*	*5*	*6*	If I can't see progress, I get frustrated
I like to stay with what I know	**11** *1*	*2*	*3*	*4*	*5*	*6*	I want to see how far I can go
I would regard myself as having good potential	**12** *1*	*2*	*3*	*4*	*5*	*6*	I would regard myself as having high potential
I tend to make decisions about people very quickly	**13** *1*	*2*	*3*	*4*	*5*	*6*	I tend to want to know people before judging them
I take risks with care and caution	**14** *1*	*2*	*3*	*4*	*5*	*6*	I take risks early and often
Whenever possible I would prefer not to rock the boat	**15** *1*	*2*	*3*	*4*	*5*	*6*	Whenever possible I would prefer to tell it like it is
The customer is not always right	**16** *1*	*2*	*3*	*4*	*5*	*6*	The customer is always right
I tend to be a procrastinator	**17** *1*	*2*	*3*	*4*	*5*	*6*	I tend to be impulsive

My work has never been as fulfilling and rewarding as I would like	**18** *1*	*2*	*3*	*4*	*5*	*6* My work has provided many opportunities for me to learn and grow
I do what my job requires but I will not be taken advantage of	**19** *1*	*2*	*3*	*4*	*5*	*6* I believe my advantage lies in doing more than my job requires
I may be too reserved in praising my coworkers	**20** *1*	*2*	*3*	*4*	*5*	*6* I may be too generous in praising my coworkers
If life is a game, I would prefer to watch it	**21** *1*	*2*	*3*	*4*	*5*	*6* If life is a game, I would prefer to play it
I like to be absolutely sure before I move	**22** *1*	*2*	*3*	*4*	*5*	*6* I believe "he who hesitates is lost"
I would like to feel more in control of my life	**23** *1*	*2*	*3*	*4*	*5*	*6* I feel I have a clear sense of purpose
I tend to focus more on the difficulties facing the world	**24** *1*	*2*	*3*	*4*	*5*	*6* I tend to focus more on the opportunities facing the world
In all honesty, I tend to do no more than what I am asked to do	**25** *1*	*2*	*3*	*4*	*5*	*6* In all honesty, I tend to add that little extra to what I do
"Always leave an escape hatch" is my motto	**26** *1*	*2*	*3*	*4*	*5*	*6* "Once decided, don't turn back" is my motto
I tend to get impatient when people don't follow instructions	**27** *1*	*2*	*3*	*4*	*5*	*6* I tend to be amazed at the different ways people approach things

I often feel suspicious of the motives of do-gooders	**28** *1*	*2*	*3*	*4*	*5*	*6* I often feel that the more I care, the more I am cared for
I have not studied how the global economy might affect my future	**29** *1*	*2*	*3*	*4*	*5*	*6* I believe the global economy provides great possibilities for me
In today's world, reality says that it is every man for himself	**30** *1*	*2*	*3*	*4*	*5*	*6* In today's world, reality says united we stand; divided we fall
I prefer to be quiet and not make waves	**31** *1*	*2*	*3*	*4*	*5*	*6* I prefer that my opinion be heard
"Play it safe" is a wise philosophy	**32** *1*	*2*	*3*	*4*	*5*	*6* "Nothing ventured, nothing gained" is a wise philosophy
With all this pressure, I am happy to maintain the status quo	**33** *1*	*2*	*3*	*4*	*5*	*6* Despite all this pressure, we need to raise the bar
People interest me but I like to stick with my own kind	**34** *1*	*2*	*3*	*4*	*5*	*6* People interest me because they challenge my mind
I believe I would be better off if I had fewer problems	**35** *1*	*2*	*3*	*4*	*5*	*6* I believe the more problems you have, the more alive you are
To feel secure is what matters most to me	**36** *1*	*2*	*3*	*4*	*5*	*6* To feel that I'm growing is what matters most to me
My job description defines what I do	**37** *1*	*2*	*3*	*4*	*5*	*6* My job description guides what I do

38							
I have felt many times that the cards of life are stacked against me	*1*	*2*	*3*	*4*	*5*	*6*	Despite many setbacks, I still feel: "If it is to be, it's up to me"
39							
There is so much I have to know	*1*	*2*	*3*	*4*	*5*	*6*	There is so much I want to know
40							
I tend to be a little too reserved for my own good	*1*	*2*	*3*	*4*	*5*	*6*	I tend to be a little too gregarious for my own good
41							
"If it ain't broke, don't break it" is my motto	*1*	*2*	*3*	*4*	*5*	*6*	"If it ain't broke, break it!" is my motto
42							
I am concerned about the future and my place in it	*1*	*2*	*3*	*4*	*5*	*6*	I am confident about the future and my place in it

**These numbers are not my own.
They come from someone who knows what he is talking about.**

Wisconsin Legislator

SELF-ASSESSMENT SCORING INSTRUCTIONS:

1. Transfer your answer for each item to the spaces provided below.

2. Add the scores for each line as shown.

3. Total all the lines (**A to G**) for an overall Thriving score.

A. $1 + 8 + 15 + 22 + 29 + 36$ =   _____

B. $2 + 9 + 16 + 23 + 30 + 37$ =   _____

C. $3 + 10 + 17 + 24 + 31 + 38$ =   _____

D. $4 + 11 + 18 + 25 + 32 + 39$ =   _____

E. $5 + 12 + 19 + 26 + 33 + 40$ =   _____

F. $6 + 13 + 20 + 27 + 34 + 41$ =   _____

G. $7 + 14 + 21 + 28 + 35 + 42$ =   _____

OVERALL THRIVING SCORE   =   _____

EVALUATING YOUR SCORE

■ SCORE: 42-63

A score in this category suggests that life is quite a struggle for you at the moment. In other words, life is tough and merely "surviving" the day feels like a major achievement. You also might feel that the future holds little promise for improvement. Many areas in your life seem not to be working, including your relationships and your job.

Your confidence level is low, which probably can be traced to a lack of purpose and direction for your life. In many ways you feel "stuck"and may even fear that this is as good as it is going to get. You also may see yourself as a victim of forces beyond your control, which could be leading to a defensive, self-defeating cycle of behavior.

Now for the good news: You were willing to complete the assessment! You are reading this book! Both of these actions require great courage when you are just "surviving." You know you want better things for your life, and you are doing something about it. Congratulations, for this is a most significant step. Now you must keep going because, whether you feel it or not, you have begun your journey toward thriving.

It is not easy to find happiness in ourselves,
and it is not possible to find it elsewhere.

Agnes Repplier

■ SCORE: 64-125

A score in this category suggests that life is clearly not what you wish it to be and you see more cause for concern than celebration. You have not lost hope, but there are too many days that are difficult and burdensome than you feel there should be. You may experience feelings of being out of control in several areas of your life, which can lead to unhealthful levels of stress and tension.

There is a good chance that you feel out of balance as you try to juggle competing priorities. Most likely you lack a clear vision of the future and are struggling with what you truly want out of life. The level of fulfillment and satisfaction in both your work and your relationships is also probably much lower than you would like it to be.

Now for the good news: You are taking action on your situation. You are aware that life is not what you want it to be, and you are doing something about it. You were willing to be honest with yourself and face reality. That shows character, a mental toughness. Keep going, for you are clearly on the road to becoming a thriver!

The happiest people don't necessarily have the best of everything; they just make the best of everything.

Anonymous

■ SCORE: 126-189

A score in this category moves you into the territory of a thriver, which suggests that, for the most part, you feel that life is working for you. You may not have everything lined up as you would wish, but you have a sense of progress and are optimistic about the future. You have an overall sense of well-being but would like to have a little more control of your life than you have at the moment.

Although you are not without problems, you feel confident that you can handle them. In other words, your perspective on life is that there is always a light at the end of the tunnel. You probably feel engaged by your work but, if not, you would have no hesitation in looking for something more fulfilling. You enjoy positive relationships but, when they are not so good, you can deal with them in a constructive manner.

In regard to the future, your orientation toward continued growth and learning is a significant asset for bringing greater order to your life. You have a positive perspective of where you are and your capabilities. This gives you wide ranging possibilities for where you can go and what you can be. Keep going; life will get even more exciting for you.

The greater the artist,
the greater the doubt.

Robert Hughes

The
Eagle's
Secret

■ SCORE: 190-252

A score in this category suggests that you are definitely thriving in most areas of your life. You have a clear sense of purpose and are moving toward the goals that are important for you. You have worked out your priorities and values and are doing an admirable job of living up to them.

To you life is certainly worth living.

You do not, however, feel as if you have "made it." You believe there is still much to accomplish and experience, and you are committed to continued growth and learning. Your relationships are satisfying and enriching, and you know how to keep them that way. Your work is also very fulfilling, but you would not have it any other way.

The effort you have made up until this moment to get your life in order will continue to pay handsome dividends in the future. The opportunities that the world is presenting for people willing to think and behave like you are limitless. Your example and influence will have a significant, positive impact on the lives of many. Keep going; life will become even more enriching for you.

Life begets life. Energy creates energy.
It is only by spending oneself that one becomes rich.

Sarah Bernhardt

WORKING WITH THE INDIVIDUAL SCALES

As you look to decide what area of your life to focus immediate attention on, understand that each of the seven scales of the Thriving Inventory, A through G, correlates with the first seven chapters of this book. In other words, A pertains to Chapter 1, B pertains to Chapter 2, and so on. On each scale your potential score was from 6 to 42. The chapter relevant to each scale has been written and designed to help you in any area where your score was low (21 or less). For example, if you scored 21 or less on scale E then the contents of Chapter 5 should serve you well. Each chapter, however, also contains insights, stories, situations, and questions that, no matter what your score, will expand your experience of thriving.

Before we proceed any further, take a moment to give yourself a hearty pat on the back. Whether you scored high or low is, in the big picture, insignificant. What is truly significant is that, through the action you have just taken, you have joined an exceptional group of people—those who have chosen to live not by accident but on purpose. You have made a statement about the direction in which your life is heading. You have taken a stand on what you want for your life. You have proven that you are not afraid to confront the truth and to forge ahead. In other words, you have clearly demonstrated your commitment to being a thriver.

Most people are willing to pay more to be amused than to be educated.

Robert C. Savage

A rabbi once said: "Some people wake up and say, 'Good morning, God!' while others say, 'Good God! It's morning!'" As we get toward the end of this chapter, therefore, it would serve us well to reflect on the difference between surviving and thriving.

To survive means to not die. The survivors in the new world of work will learn what they need to learn and do what they need to do to ensure their existence. The problem with this mentality is that if we learn just enough and do just enough so that we won't get fired, then we will be paid just enough so that we won't leave.

To thrive, on the other hand, means to get on well, to prosper. And that is the goal to which we are committed. Thriving will require, however, that we continually add to our skills, apply those skills productively, seek additional education and training, and make sure that our gifts and talents are being utilized fully or, at the very least, we are moving in that direction.

Fortunately, to do this, you don't have to move or go anywhere. In fact, you have a vast array of choices that are totally engaging and will expand your vision of who you are and what you can be. In the days and weeks to come, try the following:

■ **INVEST IN YOURSELF.** Learn more about how your field, industry, or profession is adapting to economic globalization and the new world of work. Subscribe to one or two trade journals. Read the journals for the industries in which your key customers are engaged. If you're really ambitious, take a look at some of the relevant trade journals published in other countries.

■ **EXPAND YOURSELF.** Read foreign publications. *The Times,* one of the finest newspapers anywhere, provides excellent coverage of world events from a British perspective. *The European* is another newspaper that offers an insightful look at the entire European economic community. *Time* and *Newsweek* offer Asian editions of their magazines. The *International Herald-Tribune,* although published in the United States, takes a global approach to the news. Many large bookstores and newsstands, major libraries in most large cities, and libraries in large universities offer a wide selection of international magazines and newspapers published in English.

■ **EDUCATE YOURSELF.** Buy a current atlas of the world or one of the wonderful CD Roms that have a whole encyclopedia on them. At your leisure, browse through the maps of foreign cities and countries, investigating whatever interests you the most: geography, industry, languages, religions, transportation systems, climate, and so on. What do you know about Asia, Africa, and India? Over 50 percent of the world's population lives in these areas.

■ **ENRICH YOURSELF.** At social gatherings, instead of avoiding people who don't dress or look or talk like you, step up and introduce yourself. Ask them about their culture or country. Most will be quite happy to talk. All you risk is a little initial discomfort, in exchange for some genuine understanding and connection.

Life can get away from you.
Don't be satisfied with just pumping blood.

TONY CAMPOLO

The
Eagle's
Secret

■ **INCULTURATE YOURSELF.** Take in exhibits from other countries and cultures. Go to ethnic restaurants and experience different foods. Savor the flavor of dishes that are very distinct from what "mother used to make." Visit museums and art galleries. Those history lessons that bored your socks off in high school can be fascinating as an adult.

■ **ENJOY YOURSELF.** Tune in to the Discovery Channel, the Learning Channel, public television, C-Span, or any other programming that expands your awareness of how people of other nationalities think, feel, and live. Rent foreign films, even those dubbed or subtitled. Be adventurous, try films from Asia, South America, and Africa, besides the many excellent and highly entertaining European films.

■ **AMAZE YOURSELF.** Surf the World Wide Web. Let the Internet bring you in contact with people, stories, knowledge, answers, wisdom, opportunities, creativity, outrageousness, and great ideas. Discover possibilities few would have conceived of even ten years ago.

■ **INSPIRE YOURSELF.** Read books or articles about people who changed the world. These might be inventors, entrepreneurs, writers, business leaders, scientists, political leaders, artists, or other public figures. The lives of people such as Mohandas Gandhi, Marie Curie, I. M. Pei, Igor Stravinsky, Mary Shelley, Ray Kroc, Toni Morrison, and Leonardo da Vinci will lead you out of standard modes of thinking and move you in new, unexplored directions.

Never be afraid to sit awhile and think.

Lorraine Hansberry

In my mid-forties, I returned to college and earned an undergraduate degree, while raising teenagers and working full time.

This achievement gratified me personally and allowed me to climb into a mid-level management position. The lesson the experience taught me was that I can achieve any goal by setting and managing priorities and reminding myself that I'll always be able to change and grow.

CAROL PFEFFERKORN – DIRECTOR OF EDUCATION, WISCONSIN HOSPITAL ASSOCIATION

In my first book, *Even Eagles Need a Push,* there is a puzzle: to take nine dots arranged in the shape of a square, and connect them all by drawing only four straight lines without once removing the pen or pencil from the page. The solution to this puzzle lies in thinking outside the lines, in expanding your vision beyond the imaginary box implied by the dots and drawing lines that both bring together dots and extend beyond them.

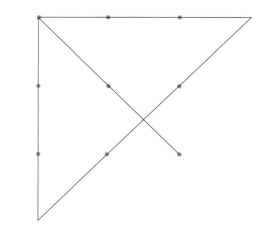

In the new world of work, thinking "outside of the box" has become a business imperative.

But that was then, this is now. Let's take a fresh look at this exercise. This time picture every dot as representing a different area of your life; within each dot is a separate and distinct set of nine dots.

**MY
PROFESSION**

**MY
ORGANIZATION**

**MY
INDUSTRY**

**MY
FAMILY**

MY "SELF"

**MY
COMMUNITY**

**MY
COUNTRY**

**MY
LANGUAGE**

**MY
CULTURE**

The ongoing challenge for each of us is how to move beyond the boundaries implied by these figures. We must learn to break through the barriers of our habits, experiences, and assumptions. In other words, if we truly are committed to thriving, we must have the courage to venture out into the world of possibilities that lie on the other side.

In the weeks ahead, therefore, no matter your current circumstances, prove that you are ready to thrive by implementing the following:

■ **ANTICIPATE THE FUTURE.** Learn more about the strategic direction of your company. Talk to your clients, supervisors, or employers about their needs. Find out about their future plans and how you could help them achieve their goals. Anticipating change prepares you for meeting your own future needs and goals.

■ **DO YOUR OWN RESEARCH.** Corporations need to invest heavily in research and development in order to retain their competitive edge. Each of us needs to research where we are and where we wish to go. Take some quiet time to ask and answer these important questions: What can you do better, more efficiently, and more effectively? How can you better serve your organization? What will be the next stage of your growth and development?

■ **BECOME FISCALLY LITERATE.** Sign up for seminars, workshops, or other opportunities that will help you understand the financial aspects of business. Learn why businesses become and stay successful. Take courses in micro- and macroeconomics. The purpose is not necessarily to become an expert but to become fully aware of how you, your company, and your country are, and will continue to be, dramatically affected by the global economy.

■ **FOCUS ON CONTINUOUS IMPROVEMENT.** Each one of us needs to become more skilled, more knowledgeable, more adaptable, and more versatile. Depending on your situation, this may mean reading books or attending lectures; or it might mean pursuing an advanced degree or taking several intensive training courses.

■ **BE TRUE TO YOURSELF.** Take time to explore ways of making a living that would draw fully on your gifts, talents, skills, and abilities. What line of work would you find truly meaningful? What would express who you really are? For some, the search may take months or years, but there is no exploration more life enhancing and rewarding.

■ **THINK BIG.** Expand the possibilities for your life. How do you want things to be? How do you envision success? What do you eventually want to be doing? How do you want to spend your time? Who do you want to be associated with? Where and how do you wish to live?

Right now what you are and where you are is the result of how you have thought and behaved to this point in your life. You will be what you will be, and go where you go, because of your willingness to adapt, to change, to learn, and to grow. Thrivers, you see, have a purpose to inspire them and a vision to motivate them, which is the most potent combination for personal and professional achievement you ever will find.

Destiny is not just a matter of chance,

it's a matter of choice;

It's not a thing to be waited for,

it's a thing to be achieved.

WILLIAM JENNINGS BRYAN

SURVIVORS FOCUS ON	THRIVERS FOCUS ON
▼	▼
■ Keeping Up With Change	■ Anticipating Change
■ Reacting To Events	■ Initiating Events
■ Playing Safe	■ Playing To Win
■ Analyzing Opportunity	■ Creating Opportunity
■ Thinking Narrowly	■ Thinking Expansively
■ Taking Stock	■ Taking Charge

HOW TO CREATE A THRIVING ORGANIZATION

- Lead by example
- Teach people how to respond to change positively
- Value people by encouraging them to learn and grow
- Motivate people by giving them the tools to expand their potential
- Demonstrate respect through frequent and honest communication
- Keep an open-door policy
- Appreciate people by listening to their ideas, suggestions, and grievances

2

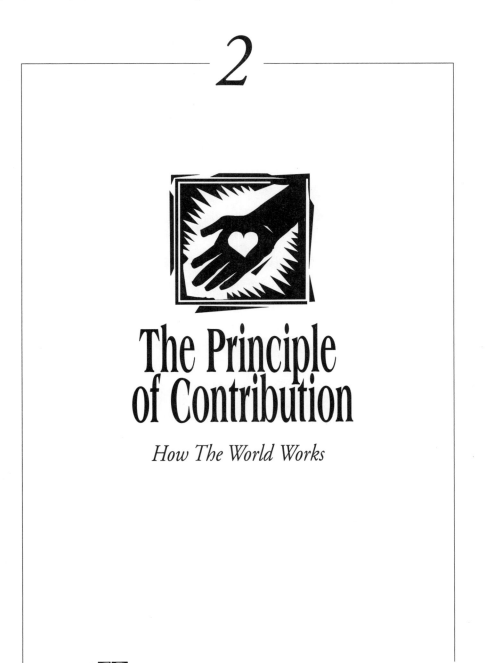

The Principle of Contribution

How The World Works

Thrivers seek to maximize their contribution —
they have a clear sense of purpose.

HAVE YOU NOTICED HOW MANY best-selling books are focused on money? Ask any group of people in any situation if they would like to make more money and, with a suspicious look, they will exclaim, "Of course! Are you crazy?"

Individuals and even the largest of corporations can't **make** money. I have a second cousin in England who spent a number of years in prison for **making** money. In the trial summary the judge said, "The defendant did a masterful job but, unfortunately for him, the government has given the Bank of England the exclusive rights for making money."

Money is obtained in three primary ways. It can be stolen, won, or earned. The first carries severe penalties. The second involves extreme odds. And the third is the result of intellectual and physical effort. The *Wall Street Journal* does not report on how much a company made, it reports on how much it earned. Earnings result from a company's ability to attract and retain customers with products and services that can be delivered profitably.

At an individual level, earnings are the reward for converting skills, talents, and energy into a service valued and recognized by employers, customers, clients, or consumers. In other words, earnings, whether corporate or personal, are compensation for contribution. The grasping of this economic reality never has been more important than in this world of global competition.

Creating opportunities for human beings to earn sufficient money to meet their immediate needs and to provide for their futures is one of the most important goals facing humanity today. A brief study of Eastern Europe and the Third World would demonstrate that economic development is their most urgent and critical priority. "It is vital that the international community recognize that the immediate need is job creation," said David Wolfensohn shortly after he was named president of the World Bank.

Economic development requires investment. Investment begins with capital. Capital is money. Money has to be earned. Unless you live with the philosophically convenient yet false notion that all people who have done well financially are charlatans, it would seem that they would have much to share and teach about how to earn money and become prosperous.

Living within your means, saving, and wise investment would be among the first lessons. But the questions left begging to be answered are: How do you get started? How do you get the money to save and invest? Here then is an answer that has proven to be the solution to many of life's most difficult problems: **Find a need and fill it.**

The budding entrepreneur, eager for independence and wealth, must first discover an outstanding need that people are willing to pay to have filled. Job seekers must understand that no organization wants to "give" them a job, but always will be interested in someone it thinks may help them succeed. Even the individual bursting with compassion for humanity is best served

Unquestionably, there is progress. The average American now pays twice as much in taxes as he formerly got in wages.

H. L. Mencken

The
Eagle's
Secret

through finding a cause, a persistent human problem to which he or she would commit the time and energy to solving.

It is frustrating how ignorance or denial of this simple premise, to find a need and fill it, is the cause of so much lack and envy. It is much easier to believe in magic answers, hidden keys, or luck. Winning the lottery is luck. The good fortune that results from diligent, dedicated effort toward solving problems and meeting needs is unquestionably earned.

Leslie Ross is an entrepreneur who has created a highly successful personal products company, Thymes Limited. But when she began, Leslie kept a tally sheet taped to her refrigerator telling her just how much product she needed to sell to feed her family, pay the rent, and keep the company going. Leslie, recently divorced and with little capital, was a one-person operation. She manufactured the products in her kitchen, packaged them in her living room, and sold and delivered them out of her car.

Knowing she had only a high school diploma and was naive about the inner workings of business, many people would have given Leslie little chance for success. But she was creative, enjoyed what she was doing, and had a sense for what was missing in the marketplace. There was a need out there and she was going to fill it. From the simplest of beginnings, Thymes Limited is now a highly profitable company with fifty plus employees and customers such as Saks, Neiman Marcus, and Harrods in London. Celebrity users of her products include Kenny Rogers, Naomi Judd, and Brett Butler.

Leslie Ross would be one of the first to acknowledge that she is fortunate. But those who know her say her good fortune is in no way a function of luck. It is clearly the result of considerable effort, persistence, and a commitment to creating products that people need and want.

Most important, Leslie was applying a fundamental principle of life! A principle that, when fully embraced, will change your life forever. It is **The Principle of Contribution**. The principle can been stated in many ways, but the thriver understands it as follows: "Before crops can be reaped, seeds must be sown; before profits can be reaped, problems must be solved; before love can be reaped, love must be shown."

In a world that is changing at breakneck speed, the Principle of Contribution has never changed, its truth is timeless. Every significant accomplishment can be traced back to a commitment to this principle.

Reflect for a moment on the people you truly admire. Who comes to mind? Your mother or father, a teacher or minister, a colleague, friend or loved one? How about those people who, no matter our own political or religious preference, we would quickly agree are admirable? Mother Teresa, Nelson Mandela, Walt Disney? Some made millions of dollars while others carried their worldly possessions in a bag. Yet something makes these people special!

The answer is no more complex than that the most admired people in the world are the great contributors to the world, those who focus on great

When Pope John XXIII was asked how many people worked at the Vatican, he answered, "About half of them."

Theodore M. Hesburgh

possibilities and move purposefully toward them. The most important people in your life are those who contribute to your life, those whose very existence gives your life meaning.

Bill Parker, a public relations executive for a medium-size computer software company, is a visionary at work and in his community. Bill has consistently worked to find ways to enhance the position of our company in the community and give back to the people in the neighborhood.

Recently Bill helped set up a program for inner-city gangs to express their needs and concerns in a nonhostile way. Together with a nonprofit foundation and local schools, he helped start a program that encourages them to communicate using computers and multimedia technology. Instead of burning down city hall to reach authorities, these kids are now using positive tools to communicate. In the process, they also are learning marketable skills that can lead to real jobs.

WILLIAM WARRICK – NATIONAL DIRECTOR, DELOITTE & TOUCHE LLP

We contribute through a simple word of encouragement or a listening ear. It might involve helping with a personal, professional, or technical problem. We contribute different things in different areas of our lives. In our families we may contribute patience, kindness, attention, and guidance to our children. At work it may be energy, creativity, leadership, skills, knowledge, or expertise.

Vicki Spina was a successful employment recruiter for many years before discovering what would be her unique contribution to life.

"My industry began changing a lot, and I wasn't happy with the changes. So I started to take some notes for writing a book but, of course, I was never serious. One evening I went to a seminar called 'Understanding Yourself and Others.' During the course of the weekend, the facilitator asked me what my dream was. I didn't think I had a dream. I was pretty afraid that I would have to come clean and say 'I don't know.' And all of a sudden I just blurted out, 'I want to write a book.' And it was funny, because I didn't know where that came from. The seminar leader said, 'Well, when are you going to have the book done? Give me a time.'

"I said, 'Six months.' I ended up going home and being all excited and getting notes together. About three months into it, I started getting discouraged and forgot about it. A few months later I went back to the seminar.

"The facilitator was talking to a young man who had half written a book on divorce. She asked him why it wasn't finished, and he said he didn't know. She said, 'Well, it's too bad because I could have really used your information. I got divorced last year.' She then asked the whole group, 'How many other people in this room have a half-written book?' I raised my hand and she asked, 'What's your book on?' I said it's on helping people with their careers. 'Oh!' she replied with great feeling. 'How I could have used that, too. It would have saved me a lot of grief.'

"I went home that night and I pulled out my book and dusted it off and said, 'Okay, if I'm not willing to do it for myself, I need to do it for others, because there are a lot of people in pain out there.'"

I know God will not give me anything I can't handle.
I just wish He didn't trust me so much.

MOTHER TERESA

The
Eagle's
Secret

When Vicki's book, *Getting Hired in the '90s,* became highly successful, a publisher approached her wanting to publish a second edition. She said, "I'm now in a position where I am living my dream. I wrote out my ideal job and I have it now. I love what I'm doing."

Great leaders, great bosses, great parents, great spouses, great friends, and great organizations all have one thing in common: They contribute to the well-being of others. Contributors, in other words, always leave the world better than when they entered it.

As my own life and career have evolved and changed, the Principle of Contribution has been a reliable reminder of what is constant and meaningful. In the early stages of my work life, I was focused solely on success, measured in terms of dollars and cents. Mine is not an uncommon story. It took my wife and five children walking out on me when I was thirty-seven for me to realize that the six people who really contributed the most to my life had just left it. Now that'll wake you up! All I knew during my intense emotional pain was that I wanted them back.

We were apart for fifteen months, which allowed me plenty of time to learn that happiness is a result of giving priority to that which you value most. I could not deny that my work played an important role in my life, but the separation proved that work did not supersede my family. The most powerful insight, however, was that it was not necessary to choose between one or the other. The answer was in developing the ability to blend them more skillfully. (We will deal with this in greater depth in Chapter 7.) In fact, the breakdown in my marriage was not caused by my obsession with work but by my wife and I not applying the principle: We had stopped contributing to each other.

Any successful relationship between two people—in other words, any relationship that has at its foundation unequivocal trust—is one where each person in the relationship is contributing, in a significant way, to the other person's life. Its source is a commitment to fully supporting each other's goals and aspirations. My wife and I needed to understand what was important for each of us as individuals and as a couple. We had to listen, and care, and encourage.

The president and CEO of a medium-size corporation shared one of the lessons she recently learned about the Principle of Contribution.

Fall 1990— Personal Belief: The richest, most powerful, and most beautiful among us are the only ones who matter. The rest of us are here to support and serve.

Fall 1991—Personal Belief: We all have a significant role to play. It is our duty to determine that role and our obligation to fulfill it. We all have a significant place in the circle of life; we must step forward and take it.

Variable: The birth of an angel, Emily Elizabeth, diagnosed with Down syndrome. Her purpose is to remind each of us that none of us is perfect, yet we all have a contribution to make.

MAUREEN GUSTAFSON – CEO, MANKATO CHAMBER AND CONVENTION BUREAU

Laugh and the world laughs with you. Snore and you sleep alone.

MRS. PATRICK CAMPBELL

The
Eagle's
Secret

The moment we accept that our contribution really matters, we begin to understand that there is an important and wonderful purpose for our existence. Deep resolve and commitment always can be traced to a meaningful purpose. When we need the resilience to handle life's most difficult challenges, a sense of purpose is our most powerful ally. It is also a sense of purpose upon which the thriver builds an exciting and meaningful future.

Mark Knopfler, the founder of the super-successful rock group Dire Straits, during an interview about his solo album, *Golden Heart*, said: "It's become important for an intelligent person to try to combat all the cynicism around today. All the cleverness in the world is not as important as addressing the soul. There are songs that just help people to live. It was a wonderful thing for me recently when a boy said: 'When all my troubles are way too much, I go home and put on your music, and they all go away.' ...It makes me feel quite good."

Taking the time to identify how you contribute now and how you would like to contribute in the future is one of the most rewarding and powerful investments of your time you can ever make. Is it easy? Not necessarily! The transformation process is rarely easy, for it takes a willingness to step boldly out of your comfort zone.

But why wait? Let's begin the process.

*Take a moment and check your current contribution
by answering the following questions:*

ARE YOU DRIFTING THROUGH LIFE, OR DO YOU HAVE A DESTINATION?

WHOM DO YOU INTERACT WITH ON A DAILY BASIS?

DO YOU BELIEVE YOU HAVE WHAT IT TAKES TO MAKE A DIFFERENCE? EXPLAIN.

DO YOU SEE OPPORTUNITIES TO CONTRIBUTE? IF SO, WHERE? IF NOT, WHY NOT?

Assess now the value you bring to your work:

MY TOP THREE STRENGTHS AT WORK ARE:

I COULD BUILD ON THESE BY:

THREE WEAKNESSES I HAVE ARE:

SOME WAYS I CAN COMPENSATE FOR THESE ARE BY:

HOW MIGHT MAKING THESE CHANGES AFFECT YOUR WORK LIFE?

In his book *Managing the Non-Profit Organization*, the renowned management expert Peter Drucker tells that when he was just thirteen he was inspired by a teacher who posed the following question to his class: "What do you want to be remembered for?" After being met with blank stares, the teacher good-naturedly said: "I didn't expect you to be able to respond. But if you still can't by the time you're fifty, you will have wasted your life." Drucker says that the question remains one of the most important questions in his life. Now in his eighties, Drucker continues to ask it of himself because, he says, "it induces you to renew yourself...it pushes you to see yourself as the person you can become."

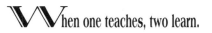

When one teaches, two learn.

Robert Half

ASSESSING YOUR CONTRIBUTION

Clarify now the contribution you would like to make in the future
by doing the following exercise: Imagine that you are sitting
in the front row of your own memorial service. What thoughts
and feelings would you like those in attendance to be experiencing?

I'D LIKE MY FAMILY AND FRIENDS TO REMEMBER ME FOR:

I'D LIKE MY COLLEAGUES, COWORKERS, CLIENTS, OR CUSTOMERS TO REMEMBER ME FOR:

THE ADJECTIVES I'D LIKE PEOPLE TO USE IN DESCRIBING ME ARE:

I'D LIKE PEOPLE TO REMEMBER ME FOR MAKING A DIFFERENCE BY:

The
Eagle's
Secret

Why is this seemingly microscopic attention to who we are and what we do necessary? One urgent reason is that performance pressures generated by the global economy are leading every organization to measure the efficiency of all resources, especially the most costly of all, people resources. Therefore, if we want to thrive in our professional lives, we need to continually assess the value we bring to those we serve, while keeping constantly vigilant about how we might increase or expand our contribution.

A colleague recently interviewed for a higher-level position. His attitude was "I have done the job and now deserve this promotion." In the interview he was asked about his development plan. He didn't have one. The individual did not get the job, and one of the reasons was his attitude.

Since the interview, the employee's paradigm has changed from advancement to growth. He later participated in an executive development program that enhanced his technical and behavioral skills. While still interested in advancement, he is now better able to thrive due to his mind-set. He is now seeking to maximize his value to the corporation through continual education. This has resulted in greater overall job satisfaction.

GEORGE ARSENEAU – SENIOR VICE PRESIDENT, HUMAN RESOURCES, ALLIANT FOODSERVICES INC.

In the workplace the quest to raise the level of contribution is not, however, just the employee's responsibility. Companies are starting to understand that asking for loyalty and commitment is absurd if employees have no assurance they will have a job tomorrow or, as has been the case for many, they have witnessed their benefits erode while profits explode. When companies start to thrive, employees want to share in that prosperity.

The Hays Group, a worldwide consulting firm, has for many years partnered with *Fortune* magazine to identify the world's most admired companies. The criteria for selection are stringent and involve not only bottom-line performance but also a company's ability to attract and keep good people. What is common to all the winners, however, is their acknowledgment that none of their success would be possible without the goodwill and commitment of their people. While this is common rhetoric, the most admired companies believe it and act upon it. They go to great lengths to ensure their employees are not only fairly compensated but also are genuinely cared for, encouraged, and respected as whole persons who have multiple demands on their time and loyalties.

For the less enlightened companies a significant new trend is proving to be, in its urgency and irony, a major wake-up call: After a decade of downsizing, the tide has turned; now many industries are facing an increasing shortage of skilled and talented people. No matter what the industry, brainpower drives it, which means that human intelligence is more valuable than ever before and is growing more so. It would be in the interests of any organization, therefore, to recognize quickly that, in the foreseeable future, the best people have a growing array of choices and will migrate to those organizations clearly and actively committed to helping them be successful in both their personal and professional lives.

There is only one thing worse than fighting with allies and that is fighting without them.

Winston Churchill

The
Eagle's
Secret

Says Kun-He Lee, chairman of the Samsung Group: "Only organizations which contribute to mankind will last; those organizations which lack humanism and morality can never become premier companies and will not endure."

The Olympic Games, as we know them today, have been in existence for over one hundred years. It serves us well to remember that we owe the revival of this spectacular event to the commitment of one man who, by seeing a need and responding to it, made an everlasting contribution. He was a Frenchman, Baron Pierre de Coubertin. An educator by profession, de Coubertin believed that what the world needed, if countries were to coexist in peace, was the "spirit" of the Olympics.

In the 1880s, de Coubertin began his quest to revive an event that had not been held for fifteen hundred years. He worked tirelessly to gain support and publicity for his cause. As seems to be the rule with powerful ideas, his efforts were greeted not only with apathy but also with considerable and surprising resistance.

But de Coubertin was not just a dreamer, he was a man of action. He spoke with such conviction about what the Olympics could do for the cause of peace and humankind that in 1896, almost ten years after he had begun, Athens, Greece, hosted the first of what is now known as the "modern" Olympic Games.

Many business experts use "war" as a metaphor for the strategies needed to compete in a global economy. I believe, however, that the world is tired of war and that continuing that symbolism no longer serves what the vast majority of people want to create: global peace and prosperity. The Olympics bring to light a distinction worthy of our deepest reflection: the desire to win versus the desire to destroy. With its ideals of contributing to the well-being of all nations, the Olympics provide a far more inspiring and appropriate vision for our times.

As the global economy gathers even greater momentum, the problems to be solved and needs to be met are multiplying endlessly. Opportunity is abundant, which means there is a game for all those who truly want to play. But all over the world, there is a rapidly emerging "Olympics" mind-set. Ever better equipped and motivated competitors are raising in leaps and bounds both the standards and the stakes of the game. Thriving will require us to be mentally, physically, and emotionally ready to contribute at the highest level.

Here are some exercises to get yourself in top playing condition:

■ **DESIGN A CONTRIBUTION PLAN.** Instead of thinking in terms of how far you want to advance in an organization, a traditional way of doing career planning, instead think in terms of what you want to contribute now, three, five, or even ten years from now. How can you influence your workplace to become more productive, enjoyable, and rewarding for yourself, coworkers, clients, and customers? In what new, imaginative ways can you contribute to your family and friends?

■ **DEVELOP A PURPOSE STATEMENT FOR YOUR LIFE.** Many people have spent literally hundreds of hours working on mission statements for their corporations, yet few have taken any serious time to discover a truly meaningful reason for why they get up in the morning. Take some time to decide what you want your life to be about. What legacy do you want to leave?

■ **ASK FOR FEEDBACK.** This is a powerful and courageous way to enhance the value of your contribution. It takes guts to ask people to evaluate your contribution, but people are impressed by those who do. People who continually strive to meet the needs of their employers, customers, and clients will thrive in the new world of work.

■ **NOURISH YOUR POTENTIAL.** Spend some time with books that enhance your sense of what is possible for your life. Sign up for a community education class that nudges you toward where you want to go. The great contributors in life often start with just a glimmer of what they might accomplish. But, through consistent action, they fan the flame, celebrating even the smallest of victories along the way.

■ **LOOK FOR NEEDS TO FILL.** This secret of success never fails those who practice it. What needs in your home, workplace, and community can you fill? Once you've found a need, do something about it. Volunteer a couple of hours a month to help others. Few things are more satisfying than making someone's life a little brighter.

A minister stopped by the side of a road to admire a beautiful farm. From the fields to the barns everything was clean, fresh, and well organized. Soon the farmer appeared and greeted the minister, who immediately exclaimed: "God has certainly been good to you, my son. You have a magnificent property!" The farmer paused, looked around, and then replied: "Yes, He has, but you should have seen it when He had it all to Himself."

The true success story
is the continuing success of the
ordinary individual who is responsive
to issues, smart with their choices,
and conscientious on follow-through —
consistently taking action to
move forward through life.
Because millions do this
to a greater or lesser degree,
the world advances and
individual greatness becomes possible.

DAVID CRISP – VICE PRESIDENT, HUMAN RESOURCES, HUDSON'S BAY COMPANY

The
Eagle's
Secret

SURVIVORS FOCUS ON	THRIVERS FOCUS ON
■ Making Money	■ Earning Money
■ Taking Orders	■ Discovering Needs
■ Giving Answers	■ Solving Problems
■ Doing What Is Asked	■ Adding Value
■ What's In It For Me	■ What's In It For Us
■ Life As A Struggle	■ Life As An Adventure

HOW TO CREATE A THRIVING ORGANIZATION

- ■ Lead by example
- ■ Have a clear mission and reinforce it regularly
- ■ Have an inspiring vision and publicize it constantly
- ■ Clarify and help employees understand the purpose of their jobs
- ■ Educate people in business literacy — the purpose of profit
- ■ Acknowledge the value employees bring to the business
- ■ Recognize good performance early and often
- ■ Encourage shared decision making
- ■ Reward the contributors — not the politicians

3

Personal Responsibility

It's 6:00 AM and You're Still in Bed?

Thrivers take personal responsibility for their own
careers and happiness — they are self-empowered.

ONE CRISP AUTUMN AFTERNOON, A HUSBAND AND WIFE DECIDED to go for a drive. It was a magnificent day, the sun was shining, the air clean and fresh, and winter seemed weeks away. As the couple drove along the country roads that surrounded their home, they marveled at the splash of stunning colors on both sides of the road: brilliant oranges and reds, deep maroons, and rich golds.

Suddenly, with no warning, two leather-jacketed motorcyclists came barreling out from a quiet and almost hidden lane. The bikers, after barely missing the couple's car, were gone in a flash. Shocked and shaken, the man pulled over to the side of the road and stopped. It seemed only seconds, however, before an explosion in the distance startled them even more.

The man immediately spun the car around in the direction from which the sound came. They drove just a few hundred feet before seeing what had happened: The cyclists had crashed through a guardrail, and dropped down the hillside, with one of the bikes exploding on impact. The man moved to climb down the hillside when his wife quickly grabbed his arm and said:

"What are you doing?"

"I've got to go down there and see if anyone needs help," he said.

"Wait a minute!" his wife cautioned. "It might not be safe. How do you know there won't be another explosion?"

The man stopped as thoughts raced through his mind. What should he do? Unwittingly he was being confronted with one of those moments that can define a life. He didn't ask for it, didn't desire it, yet there it was staring him straight in the face. Whatever he decided could have a dramatic impact on his own life, his family's, and any possible survivors down below.

He stepped over the twisted guardrail and carefully and cautiously climbed down the steep embankment. He found the bikers still alive. Suddenly remembering his cellular phone, he scrambled back to his car, called an ambulance, and soon two lucky young men were being rushed to a hospital. Did the man make the "right" decision? Perhaps. The bikers fully recovered. Then again, his wife's concern was justified. If the other bike had exploded, all three might have been killed. Like many of the most important decisions in our lives, the answer is rarely obvious.

To live is to make choices continually that shape the very essence of who we are. Every day is filled with defining moments, opportunities for our courage to be demonstrated and our characters to be built. Taking responsibility for themselves and their role in the world is, unquestionably, a key characteristic of thrivers.

To live is to make choices continually
that shape the very essence of who we are.

DAVID MCNALLY

But why is taking personal responsibility for their lives so difficult for so many? One answer is clearly that when we are confronted with adverse events and unpleasant surprises, finding someone or something else to blame provides a quick fix to soothe our hurt and pain.

Blaming others for our problems is another way of saying that we would get what we want, what we deserve, if only others would do what they should, or circumstances were different. Numerous targets for the blame assigners justify this popular role of "victim": International trade agreements, unfair competition, big business, religious fanatics, government that's too big or isn't doing enough; there's a villain for every problem.

We do need to acknowledge that there are many genuine victims. War, natural disasters, fraud can all leave people traumatized and devastated. In recent times, years of dedicated service seem to have meant nothing as organizations have downsized in an often insensitive fashion. The shock is real as many experience for the first time the unfairness of life or, as Rabbi Harold Kushner says: "Bad things do happen to good people." This is when anger and pain is both expected and understandable.

Yet there is an important distinction between experiencing pain and suffering and having an ongoing "victim" mentality in which we blame, make excuses, deny, and perform other forms of self-defeating behavior.

Cynicism and alienation may be understandable responses for the genuine victim; however, if we get stuck in these attitudes and behaviors, the ultimate price is the defeat of the human spirit. Cynicism is the cancer of the mind. It begins and spreads when we become disillusioned with the world and how we feel it should be. A newspaper recently asked its readers to compare their expectations about adulthood with their actual lives. "No matter how hard you work and how well you behave, success will always be in someone else's hands," one respondent wrote in. "Brains, ability, and loyalty simply don't matter anymore. Everything is a matter of leverage, power, and control."

Is there a cure for cynicism? Nelson Mandela, the South African leader, spent twenty-seven years in prison for his opposition to apartheid. After his release he had every reason to be a cynical man. Instead, he became a symbol of hope, reconciliation, and forgiveness and is boldly leading his country out of the shadows of a repressive past.

In his book *Long Road to Freedom*, Mandela writes: "I have discovered the secret that after climbing a great hill, one only finds that there are many more hills to climb. I have taken a moment here to rest, to steal a view of the glorious vista that surrounds me, to look back on the distance I have come. But I can rest only for a moment, for with freedom comes responsibilities, and I dare not linger, for my long walk is not yet ended."

Therefore, taking the position that success always will be in someone else's hands may be convenient in the short term, yet ultimately it is untrue. It is a statement from someone who has given up, who has handed his or her destiny to "them," whoever "them" are!

It has long since come to my attention that people of accomplishment rarely sat back and let things happen to them. They went out and happened to things.

Elinor Smith

Casey Stengel said: "There comes a time in every person's life and I've had many of them." There will be many times in our lives when we will find ourselves at a crossroads. One path says "victim," the other, "personal responsibility." We must decide which path to take. One path leads to mental atrophy, resentment, and despair; the other, to forgiveness, faith, and hope. Nelson Mandela took the latter path and survived an imprisonment that would have broken the spirit of many people.

What does it take, however, to break the chains of victimization?

The first step is **acceptance**, the ability to accept and face the truth no matter what the circumstances. It then involves **courage**, the willingness to look to the future, to have faith, to dare to see new possibilities. In other words, if we are to dream once again for a better life, there comes that time when we must let go of the past and be willing to move on. Finally it requires **action**, positive, goal-oriented action that leads an individual to becoming a contributing human being once again.

Stephen Crane wrote: "A man said to the universe: 'Sir, I exist!' Replied the universe, "[That] …fact has not created in me a sense of obligation."

Years ago I found myself in the office of Wayne Stood, president of the Evelyn Woods Reading School. Wayne had just completed interviewing a sales prospect. The man was leaving as I was entering Wayne's office. Wayne asked me what I thought of the man who just passed by. I said the man looked down on his luck and was not properly dressed for an interview.

Wayne remarked that the man had on the best clothes he could afford, used but clean. Wayne went on to tell me that the man said he had never had a break in his life, nobody was willing to give him a chance. Yet the man wasn't bitter. As they talked, Wayne said he saw a positive attitude, imagination, and a strong desire to want to be somebody. In short, he had all the raw ingredients of a potential winner.

Years later I was at a seminar in Austin, Texas, and met Wayne. I asked him about the man I had briefly met that day. Wayne said he had hired the man, and the man went on to become one of the top producers in his organization. Wayne said the man had the desire and will to win; all he did was provide him with the tools and, most important, help the man to stop seeing himself as a loser. "The day you start winning in life is the day you get tired of losing," Wayne told me.

GENE KRAJEWSKI – CONSULTANT,
CORPORATE EDUCATION CENTER, EASTERN MICHIGAN UNIVERSITY

Contemporary society, with its advertising messages focused on minimizing any form of discomfort, does not help the cause of personal responsibility. There seems to be a medication to numb every possible ache. Yet even pain has a purpose. "There are two kinds of pain," writes the author James Ryan, "and we can't escape both of them. The first is the pain of discipline. The second is the pain of regret. The pain of discipline weighs a few ounces. The pain of regret weighs a ton."

Taking responsibility for our lives means being willing to face some struggle now, whether that is getting up early in the morning to exercise, sticking to a budget to get ourselves financially healthy, saving and investing in preparation for the future, or being disciplined wherever the need is evident, because we recognize that, in the long run, we will be better off for having done so.

In the insurance business, we go through cycles of being competitive in our property-casualty lines. The natural tendency of our people (and management) is to avoid prospecting and seeing people.

During one of these cycles a new agent received a phone call regarding motorcycle insurance. The commissions are small on this type of insurance, and it seemed hardly worth the time to discuss. Nonetheless, this new agent scheduled an appointment, while his office partners laughed at him.

When the agent arrived at the appointment, he discussed the motorcycle insurance, but he also reviewed all the insurances the prospect owned. He sold not only the motorcycle policy but five other policies as well. This agent was taking responsibility for building his future.

GARY HAMMER – STATE SALES DIRECTOR, AMERICAN FAMILY INSURANCE

If the citizens of the United States should not be free and happy,
the fault will be entirely their own.

GEORGE WASHINGTON

In order that this issue of personal responsibility does not overwhelm us, however, we need to be very clear about what we can and can't do. People who assume responsibility for everything and everyone are misguided. There is an important difference between who we are responsible to and what we are responsible for. We are all responsible to others for our behavior, being honest, respecting their rights, treating them with dignity, and living up to the commitments we make to them. We do not have responsibility for others' happiness, their success, and the choices they make. We can take responsibility only for ourselves and, where we feel it is appropriate, seek to influence others. Trying to control others is an exercise in futility and frustration.

Nowhere is this more evident than in the role of parent. As I have observed my own family grow from manageable tykes to unpredictable, mysterious teenagers, I have been constantly humbled. My children have blown away every motivational theory ever discovered. And my wife and I feel we are aware, fully conscious, give-them-the-facts, go-to-the-ball-games, tell-them-you-care-everyday, God-loving, totally-with-it parents.

Never lend your car to anyone
to whom you have given birth.

Erma Bombeck

The
Eagle's
Secret

I have learned, however, that each person is indeed unique, a creation not only destined but required to follow his or her own path. You can give guidance but cannot take another's place on life's journey. The following words from Kahlil Gibran's *The Prophet* have helped me to come to terms with the limits of my power, what I can and cannot do.

Your children are not your children.

They are the sons and daughters of life's longing for itself.

They come through you but not from you,

And though they are with you yet they belong not to you.

You may give them your love but not your thoughts,

For they have their own thoughts.

You may house their bodies but not their souls,

For their souls dwell in the house of tomorrow, which you

cannot visit, not even in your dreams.

You may strive to be like them, but seek not to make them like you.

For life goes not backward nor tarries with yesterday.

After all that we have discussed, to understand and accept that most of what happens in the world is beyond our control can be quite difficult. The quest for power and the desire to control have caused more havoc and devastation than anything else. Personal responsibility is understanding that what we can and need to control is ourselves. In other words, even in the midst of great uncertainty and upheaval, we always have choices. We can choose what to believe about a situation and how to react to a situation.

The Wall Street Journal recently told the story of Suzy Kellett. Suzy dreamed of raising a family with her husband in their house in Idaho. She didn't expect, however, that the family would come all at once. She gave birth to quads. Ten months later her husband walked out. Feeling that her options were limited, she moved back to her parents' home in Illinois. To support her young family she took the first job that she could find: a receptionist at a magazine.

If Suzy was a victim only she knew it, for those who worked with her witnessed a person determined to get on with life. Suzy graduated to editing and research positions with the magazine and then, after joining the Illinois Film Office, was offered the position of agency director. Her responsibilities included luring film producers to make their films in the state. *Home Alone* and *Risky Business* were two of her success stories. Suzy is now head of the Washington State Film Office in Seattle.

What is remarkable about Suzy's story is that she managed to succeed in her professional life despite facing all the pressures typical in most working families, and her family has a deep bond because her love and commitment kept them all together. Her children knew that life without a father at home would be tough, but she left no doubt in their minds that they would make it. That Suzy believed in personal responsibility is evidenced in a comment by her daughter Gwen: "Mom's rules of thumb are: Adapt. Don't waste time. And do what you want to do."

**Sometimes you have to
look reality in the eye and deny it.**

Garrison Keillor

*Take a few minutes to reflect on some of the choices
and decisions you are facing in your life right now.*

WHAT CHOICES ARE YOU FACING AT WORK? AT HOME?

WHAT ARE THE PROS AND CONS OF THOSE CHOICES?

WHEN ARE YOU GOING TO MAKE A DECISION?

WHAT DIFFERENCE WOULD IT MAKE?

WHAT ARE YOU RESPONSIBLE FOR?

*Take some more time now to pause and complete the following
"responsibility inventory." Think about present and future responsibilities
in different parts of your life. The more specific you can be, the better.*

AT HOME:

PRESENT	FUTURE

AT WORK:

PRESENT	FUTURE

IN THE COMMUNITY:

PRESENT	FUTURE

WHAT ARE YOU NOT RESPONSIBLE FOR?

Part of accepting personal responsibility for your life also involves being conscious of the things that you are not responsible for. We simply can't be all things to all people.

AT HOME:

AT WORK:

IN THE COMMUNITY:

Each and every day, we make decisions about how to use the block of time that is the raw material of our lives. We're doing this even if we're not conscious of it. Our lives today are the result of all the choices and decisions we have made so far. Whether we consider ourselves creative people, we are, in fact, creators, the sculptors of our lives.

We have gone through significant changes in our organization this past ten years. It meant embracing new styles of leadership and transforming our approach to how we served our customers. Our success is evidence that the strategies have worked, but the process revealed many people who could not change. Some never even tried. In many ways today's marketplace is very unforgiving. People and organizations need to be adaptable and responsible if they are to succeed.

JAMES CAMPBELL – EXECUTIVE VICE PRESIDENT, NORWEST BANK MN, NA

In a future that promises more and more change, more and more challenges, and yet more and more opportunities, thrivers will have a clear sense of what they want their futures to be, what choices they have for creating that future, and what steps to take toward it. Being responsible means that you are mapping your journey, deciding on your goals, and equipping yourself to ensure you have the best chance to arrive safely at your destination. Ultimately, personal responsibility means that you are taking charge of your life and making things happen, not waiting for them to happen.

We always hear about the haves and have-nots. Why don't we hear about the doers and do-nots?

Thomas Sowell

Here are some ways to channel your creative power toward the things you can control: your attitudes and your actions.

■ **CHECK YOUR ATTITUDE.** Is personal responsibility an important value to you? Are you open to becoming more responsible? Having the right attitude is critical in behaving responsibly at work or at home. It implies a willingness to learn and grow, to admit promptly when you make mistakes, and to move on.

■ **WALK YOUR TALK.** Do the things that you say you are going to do. Let your "yes" mean "yes" and your "no" mean "no." People trust and respect those who follow through on their commitments, who get the job done "no matter what." Are you a person who can be counted on, who will come through despite the obstacles?

■ **MAKE A COMMITMENT TO YOURSELF.** Personal responsibility is not only about being accountable to others; it also means taking care of yourself and nurturing your own growth. Our growth as human beings certainly means doing what's right even when that is difficult. But personal responsibility also means doing that which brings us more joy and fulfillment in life.

■ **MAKE PLANS.** People who are responsible take charge of their destinies. Get serious about the things you want in life, from your physical, mental, and spiritual health to your retirement plans. You'll be surprised at how much more likely you will be to receive them.

■ **CONTRACT WITH A FRIEND.** Are there some things you really want to accomplish that you keep putting off? Then make yourself accountable to someone else. Pick a friend you trust and tell him or her what it is you want to do. Identify some specific, concrete steps required to get you there, including dates when you will take each step. Share this list with your friend and promise to inform him or her when each step is completed.

■ **DO IT.** Being responsible means making a decision, any decision that enhances the quality of your life. Avoid "analysis paralysis." So often we know clearly what we need to do yet we don't do it. Think of one decision you have been putting off in your life and make a commitment to move ahead. Experience the energy that accompanies this willingness to get on with life.

Life is at its best when it's shaken and stirred.

F. Paul Facult

In *Parade* magazine, Tom Seligson tells a story about the well known Mexican American actor Edward James Olmos, who grew up poor in East Los Angeles. Olmos lived with ten other family members in three rooms. His parents divorced when he was seven.

Today Olmos spends a significant amount of his time visiting kids from similar backgrounds but who are now in jail. He wants them to know that they have choices. "Some people say they didn't have a choice," Olmos tells them. "They're poor or brown or crippled. They had no parents. You can use anyone of those excuses to keep your life from growing. Or you can say 'Okay, this is where I am, but I'm not going to let it stop me. Instead, I'm gonna turn it around and make it my strength.' That's what I did."

Every time a kid conquers fear,

that's a great achievement.

Every time a person says "I'm sorry,"

that's a great achievement.

Every time someone stands up for themselves,

that's a great achievement too.

LAURA MEINE – AGE 13, ST. FRANCIS SCHOOL, ROCHESTER, MINNESOTA

The
Eagle's
Secret

SURVIVORS FOCUS ON	THRIVERS FOCUS ON
■ Blaming The Past	■ Planning The Future
■ Finding Fault	■ Finding Solutions
■ Justifying "Why Not"	■ Discovering "Why"
■ Pointing The Finger	■ Being Accountable
■ Staying Out Of Trouble	■ Taking A Stand
■ Self-Maintenance	■ Self-Discipline

HOW TO CREATE A THRIVING ORGANIZATION

- ■ Lead by example
- ■ Communicate candidly so people know where they stand
- ■ Be open about the business so employees feel like partners
- ■ Listen, be attuned to problems — business and personal
- ■ Create a "winning" environment, where people can soar beyond their normal responsibilities
- ■ Have the courage to say no, don't be afraid to say yes
- ■ Empower — give people the authority to make decisions and hold them accountable for the results

Forever Learning

When You're Green You Grow,
When You're Ripe You Rot

**Thrivers constantly reinvent themselves —
they are mentally agile and willing to risk.**

JURASSIC PARK IS ONE OF THE MOST popular movies ever made. Millions of people of all ages were enchanted by it, and it lead to a very successful sequel, *The Lost World*. Both films proved to be a surprisingly intimate and thrilling experience as the magic of special effects revealed to us the world of that awe-inspiring creature, the dinosaur. But why are dinosaurs so fascinating and, more important, why do they no longer exist?

One of the chief reasons, it seems, we are so intrigued by these "giants" is not only their enormous size but also the fact that they vanished very suddenly and quickly. One moment Tyrannosaurus Rex and Company appeared to be thriving, and the next they were not even surviving. Scientists still don't know exactly why, except there is general agreement that they were "environmentally challenged." In the emerging new world of 65 million years ago, dinosaurs became obsolete, outmoded. And so vivid is that image, "dinosaur" has now become a word that connotes a person, institution, or corporation whose time is past.

A cartoon I saw recently depicted a dinosaur convention. The speaker is saying: "I have some good news and some bad news. The good news is that the earth's atmosphere is warming up, the oceans are receding, and we're entering a whole new era. The bad news is that we have a brain about the size of a walnut."

Today we face good news and bad news. The bad news is that this period of rampant social, political, and economic change is creating major upheavals in every corner of the planet. The technological explosion and ever more dynamic global economy we have been discussing is as significant and far-reaching in its impact as the Industrial Revolution of the nineteenth century.

My father began his career in sales with *Encyclopaedia Britannica* in the early 1960s. I can recall our family discussing how amazing it was that so much knowledge could be crammed into one set of books, which took up relatively so little space. How quaint that notion appears today as we grasp the implication of what Will Hivley wrote in *Discover Magazine:* "Today a single hair-thin optical fiber can transmit the entire contents of the *Encyclopaedia Britannica* from Boston to Baltimore in less than a second."

The message is clear: In a world rocked by ongoing dramatic advances in technology and communication, those who don't adapt or change are destined to go the way of the dinosaur.

Now for the good news: As human beings we are more than capable of meeting the challenge. Unlike the dinosaurs, we have the tools to thrive in any environment because it appears that there are very few limits to our capacity to adapt, learn, and grow. And because the Information Revolution has forced a learning revolution, it is now more possible than ever to develop to our full potential. People and organizations around the world are being transformed and energized through the application of new learning technologies that improve retention, creative thinking, and problem-solving.

The dinosaur's eloquent lesson is that if some bigness is good, an overabundance of bigness is not necessarily better.

Eric Johnston

Our company has gone through more than twelve years of downsizing, reengineering, reorganizing, or whatever terminology is in vogue today for drastic cutbacks in personnel. We began much earlier than most companies so by the time it hit the rest of the country, we were well seasoned.

The company sold or stopped many products and services. We now have approximately 10 percent of the original workforce focused solely on our core business. The 10 percent who survived have certain characteristics in common. They are flexible, forward thinking, continually learning and, most important, have embraced the constant change. I saw this as an opportunity to learn new skills and broaden my knowledge.

If you did not survive, it was not all bad news. Many of the nonsurvivors found jobs that they are better suited for and are thriving. The process made us all less apathetic and we realized that having a "job for life" was a thing of the past.

LIZ POMETTI – MANAGER, SALES SUPPORT AND ADMINISTRATION,
WESTERN UNION FINANCIAL SERVICES

The willingness and desire to continue learning is a characteristic that not only distinguishes but embodies the thriver. In a marketplace that demands agility, speed, flexibility, and vision to satisfy changing customer needs and wants, only individuals who are forever learning will have the ability, knowledge, and adaptability to satisfy the changing wants and needs of employers.

A *Fortune* magazine article entitled "The End of the Job" has proven to be a rallying cry to these new realities. "What is disappearing is not just a certain number of jobs—or jobs in certain industries—or even jobs in America as a whole. What is disappearing is the very thing itself: the job. Today's organization is rapidly being transformed from a structure built out of jobs into a field of work needing to be done."

These tidal waves of change can be both dizzying and uncomfortable leading many to cry out: "Stop the world, I want to get off!" But the world won't stop, and we can't get off. Whether this ride on Spaceship Earth is experienced as a thrill or a threat will now, more than ever, depend on our commitment to learning. In fact, we need to develop a voracious appetite for learning.

For the thriver this means:

■ Reviewing past mistakes and extracting the wisdom gained from them

■ Making a commitment to taking some risks that are career and life enhancing

■ Developing a strategic plan for personal growth and development

But before we make the error of seeing learning as purely a "bottom-line" issue, let's pause to reflect on the really big picture. Although an important benefit of learning is to keep us employable, the purpose of

The world is very old, and human beings are very young.

Carl Sagan

learning is much more significant. **Learning, growing, renewing is the core process of life itself!** Learning stimulates and gives nourishment to our hearts, minds, and souls. It keeps us fresh and vigorous.

In his book *The Walking Drum*, Louis L'Amour says: "Up to a point a man's life is shaped by environment, heredity, and movements and changes in the world around him. Then there comes a time when it lies within his grasp to shape the clay of his life into the sort of thing he wishes to be. Only the weak blame parents, their race, their times, lack of good fortune, or the quirks of fate. Everyone has it within his power to say: This I am today; that I will be tomorrow."

Just as no single description conveys all that it means to be human, no simple definition captures the many different aspects of learning. Learning is a means of change or adaptation, a necessity for survival, a source of joy, and a path to personal enlightenment and renewal. In an increasingly diverse, interdependent world, learning is the bridge that keeps us connected to ourselves and to those with whom we share this planet.

"Real learning gets at the heart of what it means to be human," says Peter Senge in *The Fifth Discipline*. "Through learning we re-create ourselves. Through learning we become able to do something we were never able to do. Through learning we reperceive the world and our relationship to it. Through learning we extend our capacity to create, to be part of the generative process of life. There is within each of us a deep hunger for this type of learning."

If, right now, you are feeling some conflict here, that's understandable. Although most of us have a great capacity to learn, learning doesn't happen automatically. We're not born with a "learning gene" that automatically absorbs information, provides insights, or makes new connections on demand. We're born with the potential to do all these things, but it's our responsibility to develop it. "Personally, I am always ready to learn," Winston Churchill once said, "though I do not always like being taught."

Churchill now is regarded as one of the most important figures of the twentieth century. He was one of many adults who experienced and was victimized by shaming and punitive systems of education common to his times. Because of his failure quickly to grasp what he was being taught, compounded by the fact that he stuttered, it was intimated that he was intellectually inferior. Churchill answered these "experts" by rising to become the inspiring leader of Great Britain during World War II.

For many people, however, a bad experience in school, at work, or in a relationship leads them to resist or avoid any form of organized learning, even, in the extreme, to fight being "taught." (We'll delve more deeply into this problem in Chapter 5, "Discovering Your Genius.") The result is not only intellectual stagnation but also a deprived emotional and spiritual life. Eventually an emptiness and lack of meaning pervades their lives and they act accordingly.

A worker was heard to remark: "It's just not my day!" From another cubicle came an instant reply: "With six billion people on the planet, what are the chances that this would be *your* day?"

If learning is difficult, it is because learning means opening ourselves to ideas, and ways of doing things, that are new to us. It means going outside our comfort zones and stretching to experience and do things we have never risked before. It means embracing the confused, awkward, unskilled parts of ourselves, admitting that we don't have all the answers, and asking for help. It means being willing to rip things apart and put them back together to form new combinations.

LEARNING IS ABOUT:

- Change and diversity
- Bouncing back
- Gaining self-confidence
- Having fun
- Relating to and respecting others
- Maximizing your contributions
- Solving problems
- Rethinking assumptions
- Getting out of ruts
- Sharing your gifts
- Creativity and innovation
- Getting support and feedback
- Finding your purpose in life
- Personal satisfaction

And will you succeed? Yes indeed. Yes indeed!
Ninety-eight and three-quarters percent guaranteed.

Dr. Seuss

I work for an organization that views technology as an integral part of today's learning/work environment. The leadership has had the long-range vision of the need for computer networking among one hundred field offices. Gaining outside funding and shifting resources has put this organization in an excellent position to take advantage of the current explosion of information available on the Internet/World Wide Web. An ongoing training and support mechanism—while not perfect—has been very important in gaining staff adoption of the technology. A constant seeking of new information and "seeing beyond your nose" has led us to this enviable position.

CINDY NEEDLES FLETCHER – ASSOCIATE PROFESSOR, IOWA STATE UNIVERSITY

Because of the human propensity to be reactive rather than proactive, it is vital to repeat the fact that businesses and individuals simply cannot stop learning and expect to survive, much less thrive, in a global economy. This might be a daunting proposition were it not for the fact that nature has gifted us with the most extraordinary learning device ever created: the human brain. As with many gifts, this remarkable device is mostly underappreciated, although it seems that we finally may be waking up to its power.

Brain research in infants has demonstrated that a baby is born with 100 billion brain cells. These cells begin rapidly to make connections, which are referred to as synapses, as the child experiences the world around him or her. A baby, therefore, is literally a work in progress, a being with incredible potential. Throughout life the brain continues to restructure itself, making new connections and discarding old ones. It has been clearly demonstrated that mastering a skill, for example, alters the strength of neuron connections in the brain and its physiological composition. In other words, learning, quite literally, changes the brain's architecture!

Brain research also is teaching us, however, that learning isn't just something we do with our heads. In fact, we learn best when we are engaged in an interactive experience that taps all of our senses. "We learn 10 percent of what we read, 15 percent of what we hear, but 80 percent of what we experience," notes an article in the magazine *New Horizons for Learning*. The most effective learning comes from being totally involved rather than a passive bystander in the process. That's why Nike's admonition "Just Do It!" is such powerful advice.

Our company is going through a major reengineering. A late-middle-age mechanic was faced with learning a new computer system as part of his job. He was anxious about the prospect, as he'd never worked on a computer before. He was encouraged to make mistakes and be open with his concerns.

The results were dramatic. He bought a new PC, practiced with his grandchildren, and became one of the best at his job in a group of over fifty people. It's the attitude, not the aptitude, that makes the difference.

JOHN WILKINS – DISTRICT MANAGER, TRANSPORTATION/TRUCK LEASING COMPANY

I have learned to use the word "Impossible" with the greatest caution.

WERNER VON BRAUN

If at this stage the primary thoughts in your head are: This is all very interesting, but it sounds like an awful lot of hard work! Why would I want to go to the trouble? Well, if keeping yourself employable isn't motivation enough, then here are some practical questions to stimulate those learning juices. They are designed to help you make the connection between lifelong learning and how to get what you sincerely want for your life, your dreams, and your aspirations.

The only real failure is not to learn.

JIMMY CARTER

DREAMS

WHAT DO YOU DREAM OF ACCOMPLISHING?

WHAT WOULD YOU BE WILLING TO STUDY AND PRACTICE IN ORDER TO MAKE THE DREAM COME TRUE?

HOW WOULD ACHIEVING THE DREAM ENHANCE THE QUALITY OF YOUR LIFE?

OBJECTIVES

WHAT WOULD IT TAKE TO ACHIEVE YOUR DREAM?

WHAT STEPS ARE NEEDED TO GET YOU WHERE YOU WANT TO GO?

WHAT IS ONE ACTION YOU COULD TAKE RIGHT NOW THAT WOULD EXPRESS YOUR COMMITMENT TO YOUR DREAM?

One of the best ways to stimulate the learning process is simply to start doing new and different things. You might discover a once-convenient routine has become a boring rut. And remember, the only difference between a rut and a grave is the depth. As you work on these exercises, you will start to appreciate that actions stimulate feelings just as feelings motivate actions. Getting out of ruts gives you a new perspective and will spark your imagination and creativity.

LEARNING BY DOING:

- Involves the whole self: thoughts, feelings, attitudes, and behaviors

- Confronts us with our limitations and the consequences of our attitudes and behaviors

- Helps us break out of old habits and stimulates creative problem-solving

Knowledge is the only instrument of production
that is not subject to diminishing returns.

J. M. CLARKE

*Take a few minutes to consider some things
you have long thought of doing and which could provide some
valuable learning. Then give yourself permission to do them!*

ONE THING I'VE ALWAYS WANTED TO TRY IS:

A PLACE I'D LIKE TO VISIT IS:

IT MAY SOUND CRAZY, BUT I'VE ALWAYS WANTED TO:

AT WORK, I'D REALLY LIKE TO DO MORE:

In an era when people are changing jobs more frequently than ever and even jumping to whole new careers, the practical value of learning is clear. Yet remember, learning is more than a means to an economic end; it literally transforms our lives. Like bone and muscle, the mind thrives and grows stronger with regular exercise. With so many more of us living into our seventies and eighties, we simply can't afford to let our minds atrophy from disuse and neglect.

The *Boston Globe* reported on how John Morton-Finney, age one hundred, former teacher and the oldest practicing attorney in the United States, was recognized by Harvard University for his lifelong devotion to learning. In the eighty-six years between the time Finney bought his first book, a dictionary, at age fourteen, and Harvard's recognition, this son of a former slave chased learning with a hunger that led to eleven college degrees, five law degrees, fluency in six foreign languages, and twin careers as a lawyer and a teacher.

"We used to say there's no subject we can think of that Mr. Morton-Finney didn't know something about," recalled a former student. "He used to teach us that regardless of the system, regardless of what was going on in the world, we could make something of ourselves. And if you made it, you had to help somebody else. He said you must never, ever cease to help somebody along the way."

Do not go gentle into that good night.
Rage, rage, against the dying of the light.

Dylan Thomas

Educated in segregated schools in Kentucky, Morton-Finney became a legendary teacher at an all-black school in Indiana. A descendant of slaves who were breaking the law if they held a book in their hands, he has held fast to the printed word. "I always kept in mind that they were denied, by law and by custom, the right to read or write," Morton-Finney said. "This, to me, was tyranny. My interest in learning came from hearing that such things were denied to my people."

And just to make sure he hadn't missed anything in acquiring his five law degrees, Finney attended a constitutional law class at Harvard prior to receiving his award. "I always have a full program," he remarked. "I found out long ago there's many questions that no one can answer."

One of the most profound ways to enhance your learning is to find a mentor, an experienced person who can help you learn and grow beyond yourself. A mentor is someone who cares about you as a person and models the skills and character traits that you want to develop in yourself.

Many of us think of mentoring as involving two people in a teacher-student relationship, but it can happen in the context of any close relationship. All good mentoring relationships are two-way streets: Mentors learn from their "mentees" as well as the other way around.

An energetic and impressive woman named Nancy Meyer knows the value of mentoring from personal experience. "I've been very fortunate in having a number of mentoring relationships in my life and I know what a difference it can make," she says. In her first teaching job, Meyer developed a wonderful friendship with the school's principal. "She was an ex-nun who saw my love for children and helped me bring it out even more. She helped me overcome some of the personal blocks that were standing in my way. We are still very close."

A few years ago Nancy decided to leave teaching to launch her own mentoring business: WeMentor, Inc. "I wanted the freedom and challenge of working for myself. I also wanted to do something that I would never outgrow," she said. "When I was teaching, I felt a lot of joy when I made a commitment to really develop someone else. I've just transferred that passion into working with adults."

Meyer recalls a ceramic artist who was a battered wife before she moved to the Midwest from New York and joined a mentoring group. "Someone in the group gave her the name of a company to call and she ended up getting a project in Chicago. This woman got so creative that when she was in Hawaii for a second marriage, she landed another project! Now she is working internationally. If you set up an environment that promotes and nurtures people's souls, they will do amazing things," Meyer says.

If you think in terms of a year, plant seed; if in terms of ten years, plant trees; and if in terms of a hundred years, teach the people.

CONFUCIAN PROVERB

LEARNING MATTERS:

■ *For Organizations*

1. Learning promotes flexibility in anticipating and responding to changing customer needs and preferences.

2. Learning provides the knowledge of how to apply new technologies.

3. Learning stimulates creativity on how to attract new customers.

4. Learning inspires innovative new products and services.

5. Learning provides the wisdom and skills to manage a diverse workforce.

■ *For Individuals at Work*

1. Learning expands skills and competencies.

2. Learning is the conduit for the transfer of knowledge.

3. Learning is the catalyst for maximizing personal contribution.

4. Learning provides answers for how to relate to diverse people and situations.

5. Learning motivates effective problem-solving and creative solutions.

■ *For Individuals Personally*

1. Learning stimulates resilience and perseverance.

2. Learning builds self-confidence and courage.

3. Learning promotes a higher quality of life and relationships.

4. Learning provides a sense of purpose and meaning.

5. Learning is the source of wisdom and understanding.

In the past, learning often was seen as a hoop that we had to jump through in order to prepare for the future. It's time to start seeing it as the continual regeneration of your life today, the fuel of your existence. This might mean going back for additional schooling or training, or taking advantage of hands-on learning opportunities in your current situation. Either way, learning is the most direct route to expanding your options.

Wisdom denotes the pursuing of the best ends by the best means.

Francis Hutcheson

WHAT YOU'VE LEARNED

*Take some time now to reflect on how learning
has enhanced your life and how it could again.*

WHAT HAVE YOU LEARNED IN THE PAST YEAR THAT HAS BEEN SIGNIFICANT TO YOU?

HOW HAS THIS LEARNING CHANGED YOUR LIFE, AND WHY?

WHAT MOTIVATED YOU TO MAKE THIS CHANGE?

The
Eagle's
Secret

Name three new things you have learned about yourself or others
as a direct or indirect result of this change in your life.

1.

2.

3.

WHAT YOU COULD LEARN

WHAT IS SOMETHING YOU'D LIKE TO LEARN IF YOU HAD THE TIME AND RESOURCES?

WHAT IS SOMETHING THAT OTHERS COULD LEARN FROM YOU?

WHAT CAREER OPTIONS WOULD YOU LIKE TO LEARN MORE ABOUT, EITHER IN YOUR PRESENT JOB OR IN ANOTHER INDUSTRY OR FIELD?

WHAT DIFFERENCE WOULD LEARNING MAKE IN YOUR CAREER?

WHAT IS STOPPING YOU?

Learning is too important to be left to chance. Fortunately, there is much we can do to enhance our learning. But it does mean opening ourselves up to ways of doing things that we may normally not consider. So:

■ **CULTIVATE CURIOSITY.** All of us enter the world as curious, natural learners. A child's world is fresh and new, and they use their senses to gain direct knowledge of their surroundings. For children, learning is joyful, playful. Adults who are forever learning are more able to be spontaneous and intuitive. They combine what they know from direct experience with conceptual thought and imagination to gain self-knowledge and awareness. When it comes to learning, your "curiosity quotient" is at least as important as your "intelligence quotient."

■ **PAY ATTENTION.** Open your eyes and ears to what is going on around you. Make the effort to truly listen to others. Take the time to really hear what another person is saying and to ask questions. Understanding another point of view is one of the most valuable ways people have to learn. "Today work is about conversation; talking and listening are how knowledge workers learn, how they discover what they know, share it with their colleagues and in the process create new knowledge for the organization," wrote Allan Webber in a recent *Harvard Business Review* article.

■ **EXERCISE YOUR MIND.** Accelerate your learning process by taking a class at a local community center, college, or university in something that you've always wanted to learn. It might be another language, a musical instrument, or a new software program. Thanks to modern media technology, there are many ways to absorb new information. Not only will you expand your horizons, you will experience a whole new level of joy and fulfillment in your life.

Knowledge is proud that he has learned so much;
wisdom is humble that he knows no more.

WILLIAM COWPER

■ **BUILD SELF-ESTEEM.** Studies repeatedly have shown that people who feel good about themselves are better able to learn than those who do not. When you like yourself, you are more open, receptive, and relaxed, which are qualities or conditions that are necessary to take in and absorb new information. In short, find creative ways to be good to yourself. Make a list of things you like to do and start doing them. Learning should be fun!

■ **FIND A MENTOR.** Many people will tell you that they wouldn't have achieved anything like their present level of success if a mentor or teacher had not cultivated their growth and development. The opportunity to observe and learn from a mentor gives one a deeper appreciation and respect for the discipline, commitment, and skill required to achieve excellence in any field. The awareness of new possibilities and higher standards inspires us to perfect and hone our skills.

■ **BE OPEN.** Learning is about giving yourself more options, more choices. This requires learning from the unexpected, being willing to and desirous of embracing the strange or unknown. When we're open, we're teachable—we are not afraid to entertain new thoughts, ideas, dreams, values, or beliefs. Every encounter, every interaction and insight becomes an opportunity to be more fully engaged in our dynamic world.

If you approach learning as a duty, you won't know the joy of growth and change. On the other hand, if you approach your daily life with eagerness and curiosity, you will develop the attitudes, skills, resources, and relationships that allow you to thrive in any soil, in any season. And as nature constantly demonstrates, thriving is a beautiful thing.

Trees are believers in life.
A tree comes into life with all of its genes
and every fiber of its being literally
geared to growth, to expansion, to sharing
all that it has with everything around it.
Trees create their own environment;
they adapt, hang on, survive, don't give up.
When you move a tree out of the woods,
its natural environment, and transplant it in
the cold world that we live in, they make do
because that's the kind of being that they are.
Their roots will reach down and up and out.
When you're out there in the woods,
you haven't fully arrived, you're on the way,
you're becoming.

ROBERT HULETT – CITY FORESTER, BURNSVILLE, MINNESOTA

SURVIVORS FOCUS ON	THRIVERS FOCUS ON
▼	▼
- Sticking To The Familiar	- The Need To Explore
- Feeling Secure	- Expanding Their Potential
- Work As A Labor	- Work As A Laboratory
- Avoiding Pain	- Seeking Growth
- What's Necessary	- What's Possible
- Learning As Effort	- Learning As Life

HOW TO CREATE A THRIVING ORGANIZATION

- Lead by example
- Create enthusiasm around continuous improvement
- Demonstrate what a "learning" organization looks like
- Envision and advise employees of new skills that will be needed
- Provide state-of-the-art training
- Listen to employees about what they feel they need to learn
- Avoid micromanagement
- Challenge people to be their best
- Provide the "space" for creativity and innovation

The
Eagle's
Secret

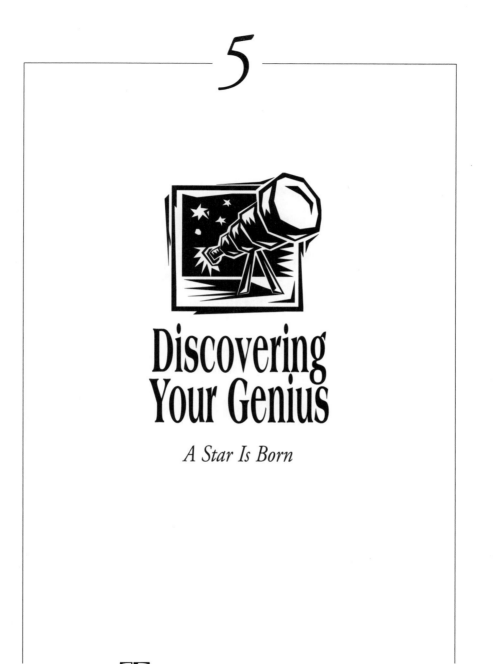

5

Discovering Your Genius

A Star Is Born

Thrivers appreciate their uniqueness —
they understand the value they bring to the world.

Elie Wiesel, the holocaust survivor and champion of human rights, tells of a rabbi who said that when we move on from this world and go before our creator, we will not be asked why we did not become a famous leader or answer the great mysteries of life. The question will be simply why we did not become the fully active, realized person that we had the potential of becoming.

You and I are entering uncharted waters. Currents of economic, political, social, and technological change are forever altering nations, communities, families, and workplaces. Humanity is being challenged to adapt and evolve in new, undetermined directions. But one thing is certain: beyond the powerful tidal waves of change there are oceans of possibilities.

You may reason, "Perhaps these are incredible times, and there may be opportunities out there for extraordinary people with talent, intelligence, and ambition. However, I'm just an ordinary person."

The idea that one has to be extraordinary to thrive in today's world causes a great many people to feel inadequate and discouraged. But, if one is willing to step back and reflect on humanity as a creation, every human being, in his or her own unique way, is extraordinary. All people come equipped with their own special genius.

If again you reason: "Genius? Who, me? Don't insult what intelligence I do have!" I could well understand. But if intellectual giants such as Albert Einstein, Madame Curie, and Leonardo da Vinci are our only models for genius, we do ourselves a great disservice. Jay Beecroft, who was vice president of human resources at 3M Corporation, summarized many years of working with thousands of people this way: "I have never met a person who at something was not superior to me. But I have also never met a person who at something I was not superior to he or she!"

Webster's Dictionary defines genius as "a strong leaning or inclination" and "a distinctive, or identifying character or spirit." Within those definitions, is it self-delusion or is it just possible that each of us might qualify as a genius? And I use the word "genius" deliberately and provocatively to claim what I believe is our birthright in the extraordinary human family. A family where, despite the billions who have existed and are alive today, it is undisputed that no member has ever possessed the exact characteristics, or combination of gifts and talents of another.

Yet the genius every person brings to life is routinely unrecognized, unappreciated, and undervalued. As a result, many settle for playing a small or minor role in the game of life. For our purposes, it is essential to investigate why.

The saddest and commonest reason is that many of us in our early years are deprived of the encouragement and support we need to cultivate our genius. Many parents are simply too busy surviving to notice the gifts of their

Genius is eternal patience.

Michelangelo

own children. Others may lack the insight, skills, or resources to draw them out. Parents whose own creativity and potential were stifled at a young age often are not even conscious of just how talented and special their children are. "All children are born geniuses," wrote the famous inventor, Buckminster Fuller, "and we spend the first six years of their lives degeniusing them."

School can be a breakthrough, but, without aware and committed teachers, a child can be "taught" but not "educated." This is a critical distinction. The word "education" comes from the Latin "educare" meaning to bring forth or draw out. To say that one has had a good education should be to say not only that one has become more knowledgeable but that one's special gifts or leanings have been drawn out, exposed, and examined, and then used as clues as to how to direct one's life. This knowledge that there is something unique about us provides a sense of purpose, the understanding that our existence matters.

While educators are beginning to recognize that children learn and grow in many different ways, there is still too little flexibility in the teaching methods that turned off previous generations of students to education. The public honors still go to the students who succeed in the classroom, which, as a celebration of hard work and achievement is, in itself, not bad. But what often is implied is that those who are not being honored are "not as bright." Even worse, some can be categorized as "slow learners," which can be not only psychologically damaging but also, in many cases, simply not true. Those so labeled, however, who have not been fortunate to learn otherwise, come to the conclusion that being "not as bright" is their fate in life. As a result, their aspirations match what they believe are their limitations which, in fact, fall far below their real potential.

Our family certainly knows the pain that is experienced when a child's talents go unrecognized. One of my daughters had considerable difficulty in school, but I had no conception of the depth and significance of her struggles. In fact, it was not until May of her senior year in high school that the extent of her challenges were revealed. The principal called to say that our daughter was not going to graduate.

Her mother and I were devastated. Surely this was not possible. At a meeting with her teachers they told us that our daughter was going to fall one credit short of what was required to graduate. Subsequently we learned that she had been skipping classes but had skipped one too many. But here was the reason: Her inability to learn in the way she was being taught at school gradually had sapped and destroyed her confidence until the risks and consequences of skipping class were far less than the pain of daily feeling more inferior and "dumb."

Through good fortune, I had recently been introduced to an organization called Square One in Minneapolis, Minnesota. They wanted to use my book, *Even Eagles Need a Push*, with their clients. The irony of the situation hit me only later. Their business was aptitude assessment of young and mature adults. The purpose was to identify not only a person's natural gifts and talents

While an original is always hard to find,
she is easy to recognize.

John L. Mason

but where they lacked aptitude. The objective was accurate and informed counseling for career and life planning.

My daughter is a very intelligent human being, and I was committed to discovering the answers to her difficulties. Fortunately, she was open to participating in the assessment. The results opened up a whole new world of understanding and opportunity. In her first private session with the counselor, his opening words were: "It seems to me you may have had a tough time in high school." My daughter was amazed! How did he know? What had he discovered?

My daughter's lowest score was in the aptitude necessary to learn successfully in the way that she had been taught. It was, in fact, almost impossible for her to grasp the abstract, lecture-style format of many of her classes. Her brain simply didn't function that way; therefore, her attempts to learn brought only the tears of constant frustration. More damaging, however, were the negative decisions she was making internally about her abilities and possibilities.

But now we had the opportunity to begin repairing this fragile ego. It began with my daughter being educated about her learning style and that she was clearly not "dumb," as her high school experience had led her to believe. What greatly helped this process were the dramatically high scores she received in several of the other aptitudes; not only did these open up many wonderful career opportunities, they also pointed out so clearly how gifted she was, her special genius! Had my daughter understood this about herself sooner, she would have been able to value, enjoy, and develop her strengths and would have had the fortitude to deal more effectively with her weaknesses.

Many of today's adults can be described as the walking wounded. Because of childhood and adolescent experiences similar to those of my daughter, they are unaware of their incredible uniqueness, their genius. But because of some profound new studies on the whole notion of what it means to be "intelligent," the opportunity now exists to heal those wounds and break through the barriers imposed by these experiences.

Leading the charge in this area is Professor Howard Gardner of Harvard University. In his book *Multiple Intelligences*, Professor Gardner explains the implications and opportunities revealed from the extensive ongoing research in which he and a group of distinguished colleagues are engaged. In summary, the research demonstrates that all human beings have considerable "Intelligence."

Most of us, however, have been measured and judged by the intelligence measured by the "IQ" test. What this test measures, according to Gardner, is "the ability to provide succinct answers in speedy fashion to problems entailing linguistic and logical skills." While the test obviously has its place, there are numerous people like my daughter who are clearly intelligent but with the kind of "smarts" the IQ test is not equipped to identify. Therefore, this singular way of measuring intelligence is now being seen as restrictive and failing to serve a large percentage of the population.

I could solve my most complex problems in physics if I had not given up the way of thinking common to children at play.

J. Robert Oppenheimer

Gardner has identified eight different "intelligences." These intelligences and examples of well-known people who have demonstrated a high proficiency in each area are explained as follows:

■ **LINGUISTIC INTELLIGENCE:** Allows individuals to communicate through language. *Example:* T. S. Eliot - Poet.

■ **LOGICAL INTELLIGENCE:** Enables individuals to use and appreciate abstract relationships. *Example:* Albert Einstein - Scientist.

(Note: The IQ test measures only these first two intelligences.)

■ **MUSICAL INTELLIGENCE:** Allows people to create and understand meanings made out of sounds. *Example:* Igor Stravinsky - Musician.

■ **SPATIAL INTELLIGENCE:** Makes it possible for people to perceive images, transform them, and re-create them from memory. *Example:* Pablo Picasso - Artist.

■ **KINESTHETIC INTELLIGENCE:** Allows individuals to use all or part of their bodies in highly skilled ways. *Example:* Martha Graham - Dancer.

■ **INTRAPERSONAL INTELLIGENCE:** Helps individuals distinguish among feelings and build accurate mental models of themselves. *Example:* Sigmund Freud - Psychiatrist.

■ **INTERPERSONAL INTELLIGENCE:** Enables individuals to recognize and distinguish among others' feelings and intentions. *Example:* Mohandas Gandhi - Leader.

■ **NATURALIST INTELLIGENCE:** Allows people to distinguish among, classify, and use features of the environment. *Example:* Charles Darwin - Naturalist.

Gardner argues eloquently and forcefully that there is plenty of evidence that success in the world beyond school is not the exclusive domain of those with superior logical and linguistic intelligence. For example, as we shall identify more clearly in Chapter 6, in the new world of work, where teamwork is essential, interpersonal intelligence is a powerful asset. This new knowledge has tremendous implications for our personal and professional lives and for our ongoing education and training.

First and foremost, this knowledge allows us to reevaluate where we have put ourselves on the "intelligence scale." If we discover that our intelligences are other than those that traditionally have been acknowledged as important, we can use this new discovery as a springboard for opening up a whole range of new possibilities for our lives. When our family examined the discoveries my daughter had made about her natural aptitudes and compared them with the multiple intelligences model, the spatial (she is very artistic), kinesthetic (she is a good athlete), and interpersonal (she is excellent with people) intelligences were clearly evident in her. Gardner says, however, that each of us is, in fact, a combination of all the intelligences and it is that very combination that defines our uniqueness.

"It is of the utmost importance that we recognize and nurture all of the varied human intelligences," says Professor Gardner. "If we can mobilize the spectrum of human abilities, not only will people feel better about themselves and more competent, it is even possible that they will also feel more engaged

To be upset over what you don't have
is to waste what you do have.

Ken S. Keyes, Jr.

and better able to join the rest of the world community in working for the broader good. If we can ally them to an ethical sense, we can help to increase the likelihood of our survival on this planet, and perhaps even contribute to our thriving."

Perry Wilson, the founder of the "If I Had a Hammer" project, is a marvelous example of what it truly means to be intelligent. Through the building of a simple house, Perry's program teaches kids from ten to four-teen that they are intelligent, worthwhile, and have something important to contribute. I first learned about Perry's extraordinary story when he was being interviewed on the radio. I then had the privilege of speaking with him on the telephone; subsequently, this very modest man sent me some information about his life and work.

Perry was labeled "dumb" right into his adult years. He can trace it back to failing fifth grade. That was when his self-esteem and belief in him-self were crushed. Not only that, he had to prepare for the punishment he was sure to get at home. Instead, his father sent him out into the backyard with the task of building a tree house. For a reason that he would discover only many years later, the math that was so difficult in school seemed to make perfect sense as he measured the lumber for his project.

Perry made it through high school and was even accepted into college, but it was because of his basketball ability not academic skills. When his athletic skills eventually were not enough to make up for poor grades, he turned to carpentry, where he felt confident and worthwhile. That is when he also began a journey of self-discovery. Perry learned that not only did he have dyslexia, which causes words to appear backward, but he also suffered from convergence insufficiency, which made them appear double. This began to explain why his school years had been a nightmare.

As a carpenter his life was normal or, more correctly, as normal as that of anyone who moves from one job to another. The son of a friend, however, helped him realize that his destiny might be different and that his own failures could be an ideal foundation upon which others could build their success. It began when Perry noticed that this fifth-grade boy was having trouble in school. Perry remembered how his own father had responded to his struggles and hoped the same remedy would work for this boy. It did, and another tree house became a symbol for human potential.

Perry Wilson realized that there were thousands of children who needed the same help and encouragement that he had given to his young friend. He decided to become an educator, but using his own style and on his own terms. He knew that building a tree house taught elements of math, science, and engineering, with carpentry thrown in for good measure. More important, it developed a sense of self-worth and the feeling of accomplishment.

He began his quest to bring his method of teaching kids to the educational community. But with no credentials and with little credibility, he was to experience very lean times. He persisted through years of rejection until

Only two kids enjoy high school ... One is the captain of the football team. The other is his girlfriend.

Letter to Ann Landers

an article in the *New York Times* provided a break. He was asked to go to Louisville, the very place where he had failed fifth grade, to demonstrate what he was all about.

Perry proved his point, but no additional invitations followed. It was not until after he had virtually given up that the major breakthrough came. A friend who Perry had asked for work saw a video of his tree house project. "You can't work for me," his friend told Perry. "You have got to make your project work!" Perry hit the streets again.

Today he has found his guardian angel. With the support of Home Depot, the giant hardware retailer, If I Had a Hammer is now moving all across the United States. And with the help of many committed volunteers, it is reaching thousands of young people who might, like Perry, have gotten lost in the cracks of the educational system.

As Perry Wilson starts to broaden his vision to projects that include computers and suspension bridges, he recalls the professor who told him that he didn't have the mental capacity for anything other than manual labor. "I carry so much baggage from my educational wounds," he says. "But I look in the eyes of these kids and I know I'm connecting with some of them."

I have been waiting to tell for several years how three people helped me to become what I am today. My mother, my father, and my sixth-grade teacher. My family is African American. My parents are not wealthy; however, their gift of providing for me the best experiences that they could afford gave me a life filled with rich values and high goals.

They reinforced that I could accomplish anything that I wanted to accomplish. They supported my educational efforts and were always a ready source of help and encouragement when I raised my children. They enjoyed being a source of aid and strength to those in need. Their love is supreme.

My sixth-grade teacher was the person who developed the creative force in my life. He taught our class how to accept the differences in others. He taught us to play fairly and have fun. From him I learned to write creatively. I also learned to research a topic with passion. He gave me a vision for reaching goals. When our class did an in-depth study of China, I determined that one day I would visit China. This I did in the summer of 1986.

I attribute my zest for life, creativity, and seeing beyond the reality of the present to my sixth-grade teacher, Louis Sarlin.

LAURA DULAN – ASSOCIATE DIRECTOR
BUSH PRINCIPALS' PROGRAM, UNIVERSITY OF MINNESOTA

Life is amazing; and the teacher had better prepare himself
to be a medium for that amazement.

Edward Blishen

The
Eagle's
Secret

Your genius, your special talents and abilities, were given for you to use, not to lose to a false set of beliefs and assumptions about yourself. Your light is meant to shine as is the light of all humankind. What would the night sky be like were it not for the billions of stars parading their brilliance? Sometimes, however, we need to remove the clouds that are blocking our view.

Reflect for a few moments as to what some of those clouds might be.

HOW OFTEN DO YOU DESCRIBE YOURSELF AS "DUMMY" WHEN YOU FIND IT DIFFICULT TO GRASP SOMETHING NEW?

DO YOU REGARD YOURSELF AS TEACHABLE?

WHAT IS THE BEST WAY FOR SOMEONE TO TEACH YOU?

HOW DO YOU BEST LEARN?

CHART 1

Here are two simple yet revealing exercises I have used in my seminars. They are designed to help you begin to identify your genius. In Chart 1, moving horizontally from left to right, list six things you're really bad at, six things that are difficult for you, and six of your greatest weaknesses.

What are you not good at?	What do you find difficult to do?	At what do you have no ability?

CHART 2

Now you're ready for Chart 2. List six things you're good at, six things that are easy for you, and six of your special abilities.

What are you good at?	What do you find easy to do?	What is one of your special abilities?

Which chart was easier for you? If it was the first one, you're in good company. Virtually everyone who does this exercise finds it far simpler to find fault with themselves than to admit to having strengths. Many people struggle to fill in all the spaces on Chart 2, but they tell me they need extra paper to do full justice to Chart 1!

How do we defeat these nagging voices of self-deprecation? First, we stop assuming that they are right. Second, when we catch ourselves dismissing, diminishing, or discounting by thought or word someone's genuine praise and encouragement, we simply say "thank you!" and then take a moment to reflect on why we're getting this positive feedback.

Yet this is only the beginning. Because genius wears so many faces, we must continue the process of identifying our unique gifts and talents. Discovering our genius is not something we do suddenly or all at once. Most often it is a gradual process whereby our talents are manifested or revealed to us through experiences like my daughter's. We have to look and listen carefully for the clues. Sometimes the clue comes in the form of external recognition. Other times it comes from the deep sense of satisfaction we get from a job that we enjoy, that is "strangely" fulfilling.

But if you need a bottom-line, no-nonsense reason for discovering your genius, it is this: Being fully aware of your particular gifts and talents, the

Confidence, like art, never comes from having all the answers; it comes from being open to all the questions.

EARL GARY STEVENS

characteristics, aptitudes, and qualities that define you, is critical for thriving in the new world of work. The greater reward, however, is more encompassing and important than being employable. One of the greatest fortunes in life is knowing what you are good at and love to do, and making the choice to do it.

I started work for this company thirty years ago as a machine operator. I strived to do the very best job I could. I watched and learned from others and accepted every challenge as a stepping-stone to better myself, my family, and my company. I own this company now. I believe the most important ingredients were common sense, teamwork, good working conditions, benefits, open-door policy, and communication. Today's workplace may be different, but I believe the same things apply.

Of course, the above story took many turns through the years, but I believe I got the opportunity to advance to a position to purchase the company because I held firm to what I thought was right for the company's sake, the employees' well-being, and my peace of mind.

ROY BOESER – PRESIDENT, METAL FABRICATING COMPANY

If you are unhappy in your present job or do not feel fulfilled, then take time to assess what is going on and to explore a course of action. For some people, it takes a major crisis to begin this process, perhaps the loss of a job or being passed over or demoted. Though it may not feel like it at the time, any of these events can serve as a catalyst to reflect on who you are and what you need to do.

Reflect on the following questions and relate them to your own life.

■ DO YOU COME UP WITH IDEAS QUICKLY AND EASILY?

If you respond to problems and situations with an abundance of ideas, then you have a creative, expansive imagination. This is a huge asset in any number of professions but it causes quite a problem when it has no outlet. The very energy that gives you that inexhaustible supply of ideas is not meant to be used on orderly, logical tasks. If you continually have to hold back your ideas with no opportunity to express them, then there's an excellent chance you're in the wrong job.

Rebecca was brought up in a home where job security was one of the highest values. Both parents came from poor backgrounds and were averse to taking risks of any kind. All her life she was steered toward getting a job where the risk of being laid off was minimal. In most cases this means working for the government. She succeeded but at the same time began dying inside.

Wherever she turned she could see better ways to do things, to improve the way her department served the public. Her ideas, however, were met by a rigidity and philosophy of "don't rock the boat." Her spirit was becoming so crushed that Rebecca had to decide whether the need to find an outlet for her ideas was more important than her parents' advice to "find a job for life."

It seemed as if the instant she was committed to making this decision an opportunity presented itself that met both needs. A movement had begun to "reinvent government," and volunteers were being recruited to serve on various task forces. The profile of the volunteer being sought was a creative, straightforward, protect-no-sacred-cows type of individual. Rebecca knew in her heart that was who she was.

Today Rebecca's job is more secure than ever not because she works for the government, but because she has built a reputation for generating ideas that vastly improve the efficiency and effectiveness of her department.

It is never too late to be who you might have been.

George Eliot

If you identify with Rebecca, take a moment to list the jobs,
positions, or professions that would reward your creativity.

JOB	POSITION	PROFESSION

■ ARE YOU COMFORTABLE MAKING QUICK DECISIONS?

If you can piece together bits of information rapidly and like to act promptly on what you see, then you will be quite frustrated in any situation where the pace is deliberate and thorough analysis is the norm. Decisiveness in forming diagnoses, arguments, and strategies, like creativity, needs an outlet.

From the time he could remember, Ray was curious about why things were the way they were. His inquisitiveness ultimately led to a career in research and development with a major international corporation. Although Ray became a highly valued employee, there was something unfulfilling in the routine of his daily work.

Ray decided that perhaps his curiosity should be directed inwardly to find out what might be missing in his life. Through a career planning process, which included an aptitude assessment, Ray discovered that although he had an intense desire to know why things worked, he was not motivated to be the person who made the breakthroughs. He also learned that his most valued role on the team was as the unelected mover and shaker, the person who prevented projects from getting bogged down in analysis paralysis.

Ray realized that he enjoyed being a leader and decided he wanted to move into management. Combining his respect for the importance of the research and development function with his ability to assimilate facts and make decisions quickly, Ray now happily heads up the very department in which his previous role had been unfulfilling.

*If you identify with Ray, take a moment to
list the jobs, positions, or professions that would allow
you to make full use of your leadership abilities.*

JOB	POSITION	PROFESSION

■ **HAVE YOUR MOST SUCCESSFUL DECISIONS BEEN BASED ON GUT FEELINGS OR LOGIC?**

If you automatically organize information into patterns, sequences, and classifications, and reach conclusions through a deliberate, orderly thought process, then you have strong logical aptitudes. Any environment that does not permit careful analysis will be extremely uncomfortable for you.

Jean took the first job offered to her out of college. An advertising agency was looking for an office manager who could bring some order to its chaotic environment. The job was immediately appealing as Jean was a methodical person who valued having things in order. Her relief at having an income, however, prevented her from asking questions about who these people were, their priorities, or how much authority would be given to her.

Within thirty days she felt like she was working in the middle of a "popcorn" machine. Ideas, projects, and people were exploding all over the place simultaneously. Decisions were made but recanted sometimes within hours. She was being pulled in several directions at once, and there were no clear lines of responsibility or authority. The stress began to take its toll.

Despite her fears, Jean decided to resign. The head of the agency was surprised and disturbed, for everyone liked Jean and felt that she was doing a good job. He was the type of person Jean could trust so she was honest about why she took the job and why she now had decided to quit. He then surprised Jean by asking her what job might suit her gifts and talents best.

Today Jean manages all the customer and prospect databases of the agency and reports only to the president. Her organizational ability is bringing a focus and direction to the agency's marketing efforts and its clients. Her thoughtful approach and attention to detail has earned her wide respect with her colleagues and within her industry.

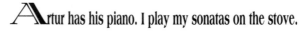

Artur has his piano. I play my sonatas on the stove.

NELLA RUBINSTEIN

The
Eagle's
Secret

If you identify with Jean, take a moment to list the jobs, positions, or professions that would respect and value your patience and thoroughness.

JOB	POSITION	PROFESSION

■ DO YOU LIKE TO USE YOUR HANDS WHEN YOU WORK?

If so, you have a high degree of the aptitude that drives you to create physical, tangible things. Research shows that of all the abilities that have been studied, this is the most urgent and compelling to the person who has it and the most disruptive if it's ignored. People who have this drive but don't use it in their everyday work constantly fight feelings of restlessness and frustration.

Larry, the minister of a rapidly growing church, by all outward appearances had every reason to be happy with his career. He believed in his work and was very successful at it. Yet he felt dissatisfied. Larry discovered that he had an extremely high aptitude for creating physical objects but his work as a minister was making no use of those abilities. The result was nagging frustration. Once Larry understood the cause of his tensions, however, the remedy quickly followed.

On parishioner calls, he began to ask if people could use his help with small repairs around the house. The requests came pouring in, and Larry soon realized that these physical tasks would become a highly valued part of his ministry. Larry is now happier and more fulfilled, which also has resulted in him becoming a much more effective minister.

All men who have turned out worth anything
have had the chief hand in their own education.

Sir Walter Scott

*If you can identify with Larry's story, take a moment to
list the jobs, positions, or professions that would increase the
opportunities to use your skills as a craftsman.*

JOB	POSITION	PROFESSION

■ ARE YOU MOST COMFORTABLE WORKING BY YOURSELF?

If you do your best work alone and prefer to concentrate on a single task, you tend to be a more subjective person. If you need a lot of variety in your work, enjoy sharing tasks and projects, and want a high degree of involvement with other people, you are a more objective person.

If you are subjective, you have a powerful need to focus on what you're doing. You tend to feel stressed, distracted, and even threatened if your work involves wearing many hats or requires a lot of interaction with people. But if you are more objective, that Lone Ranger approach is boring. You like having lots of balls in the air at once and plenty of dialogue with your colleagues.

Tina was a very successful telemarketer. So successful that her company made her a sales manager supervising eighteen people. But it wasn't long before Tina began to struggle. She was waking up at night worrying about the performance and personal problems of the people in her group. She became so anxious and distracted at home that her marriage and family suffered. In short, this person who had been thriving in her job was soon fighting to survive.

Her problem was that the very qualities that made her so effective in sales were completely wrong for being a manager. Her subjectiveness dictated focusing tightly on her own work, while her position as manager demanded exactly the opposite. When she realized this, Tina asked to be reassigned to her former position, where, in spite of the loss in status, she is immeasurably happier.

Every great mistake has a halfway moment,
a split second when it can be recalled and perhaps remedied.

Pearl S. Buck

Are you like or unlike Tina? Take a moment to list those jobs, positions, or professions that would make the most of your style of working.

JOB	POSITION	PROFESSION

Tina's experience points to a widely held point of view entitled "No Pain, No Gain." In other words, if it doesn't hurt, if it feels right, then perhaps it doesn't have as much value! Carried too far or misinterpreted, this philosophy can lead people to live their entire lives missing what they were put on earth to do.

On the other hand, just doing what is enjoyable, satisfying, or natural is not all that is required to be successful. It still takes commitment and discipline to achieve excellence in any field. The lesson, however, is that your gifts and talents are the tools with which you shape your life. Don't let them gather dust and rust. Appreciate and value them. Polish them. Learn how they work and what they can do for you.

Too much of a good thing can be wonderful.

Mae West

Here are some practical ways to start cultivating your genius today:

- **LOOK FOR PATTERNS IN YOUR LIFE.** Although you may not have truly valued your gifts and talents, they have surfaced from time to time throughout your life. As you review the events of your life, look for the threads of continuity running throughout. What have you consistently enjoyed throughout your life? What talents have you been praised for? What accomplishments are you most proud of? Answering these questions will put you on the right path.

- **PLAY GAMES.** Your natural gifts and talents are most visible when you are feeling relaxed, spontaneous, and the most "yourself." Giving yourself the opportunity to let go, to play, opens the door to discovering new creativity and new passions.

- **TRY SOMETHING NEW.** Break out of established patterns of doing things. What have you assumed you're not good at but would love to try? Do at least one new thing every month. Think of something you've always wanted to do and do it. If you fail, make a mistake, get laughed at, feel embarrassed, so what! Fears like these keep people mired in mediocrity.

- **BE HONEST ABOUT WHAT YOU LOVE.** What do you feel passionate about, what do you have fun doing? I believe that what you love is what you were made to do and what you were made to do is what you have an aptitude to do. Have the courage to admit what you love and your genius will burst through.

■ **SHINE YOUR LIGHT.** Once you identify your genius, find a comfortable way to let other people know who you are and what you do exceptionally well so that they can call on your gifts and talents. If you don't belong to a professional association, join one. Ask some questions at a meeting or volunteer to sit on a committee. Or demonstrate your expertise by writing an article for your employee newsletter.

■ **DEVELOP IDEAS.** Get in the habit of spending fifteen minutes a day listing ideas on how to improve your personal and professional life. At first your mind may be blank, but with time insights will begin to appear until, if you are disciplined in this process, a flood of ideas will present themselves. Don't censor the ideas because they seem too large or small, impractical or unreasonable. Remember, George Bernard Shaw said: "All progress depends on the unreasonable man."

For over a decade, I have served on the board of directors of Perspectives, Inc., a not-for-profit, human service agency in Minneapolis, Minnesota. Perspectives has created and developed many powerful programs to assist families in need. A wonderful group of professionals, ably assisted by specially trained volunteers, provides a broad range of services to high-risk families and homeless women and children.

Over the years I have heard stories of struggle, injustice, and heartbreak that have left me breathless and in despair. But then I have witnessed these same people transcend the seemingly insurmountable barriers of their backgrounds and start to live powerful and effective lives. The transformation always began, however, with the discovery that each and every human being is special.

My involvement with Perspectives has proven to me time and time again that appearances mean nothing, that everybody has a unique genius waiting for the right moment, for just the right encouragement to break through.

Our deepest fear is not that we are inadequate.

Our deepest fear is that we are powerful beyond measure.

It is our light, not our darkness, that most frightens us.

We ask ourselves, Who am I to be brilliant, gorgeous,

talented, fabulous? Actually, who are you not to be?

Your playing small doesn't serve the world.

There's nothing enlightened about shrinking

so that other people won't feel insecure around you.

We are all meant to shine, as children do.

We were born to make manifest

the glory of God that is within us.

It's not just in some of us; it's in everyone.

And as we let our own light shine, we unconsciously

give other people permission to do the same.

RAINER MARIA RILKE

SURVIVORS FOCUS ON	THRIVERS FOCUS ON
▪ People As Ordinary	▪ People As Extraordinary
▪ Limitations	▪ Great Expectations
▪ Meeting Standards	▪ Setting Standards
▪ Making Excuses	▪ Making Commitments
▪ Getting Through	▪ Breaking Through
▪ Hiding Out	▪ Shining Out

HOW TO CREATE A THRIVING ORGANIZATION

- Lead by example
- Identify strengths of employees and develop them
- Match people to jobs that utilize their gifts and talents
- Help all employees develop career paths — visions for their futures
- Be flexible with teaching methods — recognize different learning styles
- Get people excited about their potential
- Place a premium on personal development
- Create opportunities for people to win often
- Celebrate victories early and publicly

6

A Question of Trust

She's Your Brother

Thrivers work in harmony with others—
they respect and honor differences.

CHARLIE BROWN'S FRIEND LINUS confided in his big sister, Lucy, that he wanted to be a doctor when he grew up. "You a doctor," Lucy answered, "you could never be a doctor! You know why? Because you don't love humankind!" "I do too love humankind!" Linus responded. "It's people I can't stand!"

If there is one dominant trend that the global economy has clearly revealed, it is this: At the end of the line, it is always people who make things work. Technology is a tool, people the artisans. It is not enough to understand technology, you have to understand people too, how they think, feel, and act. Success is clearly the result of the cooperation and collaboration of diverse groups of people with a clear and common purpose.

Just as a flourishing ecosystem is a reflection of nature's amazing diversity, organizations today must nurture a wide variety of human talent to flourish in the markets of the world. Harmoniously blending different personalities, ethnic backgrounds, and cultures is no longer an option, it is a core strategy of the thriving organization. At an individual level, respecting and honoring the differences in others is a primary characteristic of those who will thrive in the new world of work.

Throughout history, however, the nobility of those ideals and the reality of human interaction have been somewhat at odds. In fact, a statement by the Roman emperor Marcus Aurelius over two thousand years ago makes us wonder if there has been any growth at all: "I am going to be meeting people today who talk too much, people who are selfish, egotistical and ungrateful." The surprise is in his conclusion: "But I won't be disturbed, for I can't imagine a world without such people."

Although Marcus Aurelius appears to have been a very wise man, it would be safe to say that he could not have dreamed of the complex world we know today. In fact, looking back just a few short years to the work environment of our grandfathers will demonstrate how today's workplace is strikingly different from theirs in several significant ways. Some will notice immediately that I said grandfathers not grandmothers. Why? Because, apart from the special circumstances generated by World War II, only in the most recent generation have women made up such a large proportion of the permanent workforce that they do today.

Today women are ascending through the ranks of management with perspectives and values that dramatically influence business decisions and corporate cultures. But the growing impact of women in the workplace is just one of the glaring changes we are witnessing. Today's diverse workforce also includes people who are different from us in age, education, personality, lifestyle, physical challenge, ethnicity, and geographic origin.

I'm a citizen of the world.

Sylvia Beach

The
Eagle's
Secret

It might, therefore, not be too far-reaching to say that in a world often torn apart by interracial tensions and violent intolerance, there may not be a more ideal place for people to learn to get along with one another than at work. Why? Common goals, the interdependence intrinsic to any organizational structure, the shared benefits that come from a successful enterprise, and the sheer joy and sense of satisfaction that comes from being a part of a synergistic team are just a few of the reasons and the incentives.

Many corporations already have taken enormous strides in this direction. When the Ford Motor Company directed its engineers to design a vehicle to appeal to the global marketplace, it was a huge risk even for this automobile giant. Realizing that Detroit was no longer the center of the automobile universe, executives looked beyond borders, finally bringing many types of people together to create and build what their marketers would call the "World Car." What was their purpose and motivation? Clearly, to better meet the increasing demands of an ever-more diverse group of customers. Designing a World Car, however, required a paradigm shift of enormous proportions.

Managers at Ford began by dividing the tasks between Europe and the United States, based on the strengths of each engineering team. The British engineering center designed the brakes and suspension, engine installation and calibration, and led the interior design team. The Germans designed the four-cylinder engine and manual transmission. They also led the exterior design team. U.S. engineers in Detroit were charged with engineering the V-6 engine, automatic transmission, air conditioning, and power steering.

It may have been the huge conglomerate, Ford, who built the World Car. But it was people working together who pulled it off. These very different individuals from two sides of the Atlantic grew to trust each other enough that, in spite of their differences, they completed a mammoth project that ended up being profitable for all involved and set the stage for the future.

In the new world of work, to accomplish our goals and objectives, we have no choice but to find creative ways to get along with others. We can't do it alone. If prejudice, in any form, is a stumbling block, it now has an economic cost that very few organizations can afford. Ellis Cose, author of *The Rage of a Privileged Class,* gives us the big picture when he says, "It is going to be awfully hard to forge a globally competitive workforce if the races can't learn to work together."

Ernest H. Drew, the CEO of Hoechst Celanese, one of the giants of the chemical industry, began to understand the cost of not appreciating that a diverse workforce actually meant diverse gifts and talents when attending a conference for the company's top 125 officers, mostly white men, who were joined by 50 or so lower-level women and minorities. *Fortune* magazine related what happened: The group split into problem-solving teams, some mixed by race and sex, others all white and male. The main issue was how the corporate culture affected the business and what changes might be made to improve results. When the teams presented their findings, a light clicked on for Drew.

The company that can demonstrate that it is blind to color, gender, age, and culture will have the greatest success and appeal to the broadest population.

Ted Childs

"It was so obvious that the diverse teams had the broader solutions," he recalls. "They had ideas I hadn't even thought of. For the first time, we realized that diversity is a strength as it relates to problem solving. Before, we just thought of diversity as the total number of minorities and women in the company, like affirmative action. Now we knew we needed diversity at every level of the company where decisions are made."

What happened when Hoechst applied the team's solutions to the company's real world of work? Productivity surged. A division that had lost money for eighteen straight years began to make a profit, as the team cut costs, improved quality, and concentrated on niche markets. A Hoechst executive credits the new workforce mix for the turnaround. "We tried everything for so many years, but the business did not perform better until we had a diverse management group."

Varieties of people do more, however, than enrich a workplace, they enhance the experience of life itself! Can you imagine travel being anywhere near as exciting or appealing if the people you met when you went to Europe, Asia, or Africa were exactly the same as those you left behind? "Travel is fatal to prejudice, bigotry, and narrow mindedness," said Mark Twain "broad, wholesome, charitable views cannot be acquired by vegetating in one little corner of the earth."

Respect is one of the greatest gifts you can give to another human being.

ARMIDA RUSSELL

One of the greatest gifts my parents gave to me was the advice: "See the world before you settle down." By the time I was twenty-two I had traveled through much of Europe, the United Kingdom, and North America. Even with that limited experience, I returned home with a deep appreciation that there were other ways of thinking equally valid or superior to my own, and that it was other people and their diverse cultures that made the world such a fascinating place in which to live.

If we are to thrive, however, valuing and appreciating others must go beyond being a noble intellectual exercise. It requires that we learn how to encourage and motivate others and help bring about the unique contribution that only their gifts and talents can make. In other words, while honoring the differences in others is a wonderful ideal, our desire to cooperate must be matched with our ability to collaborate.

An unwillingness to do so has dire consequences. In their insightful book *When Smart People Fail* authors Carole Hyatt and Linda Gottlieb report that the number one reason people do not achieve their goals and dreams is their inability to get along with others. Or, as Ivan Seidenberg, CEO of NYNEX Corporation, put it bluntly in a recent *Wall Street Journal* article: "Being a pain in the neck is an absolute prescription for failure."

Hyatt and Gottlieb define the inability to get along with others as having "poor interpersonal skills" or underdeveloped "social intelligence."

What are "interpersonal skills" and how do we develop them?

To be skillful is to be able to do something well and to be resourceful. It is knowing how and what corrective action to take when what you want and the result you are getting are not matching up. With people, it means that if what you are communicating is not being accepted or "bought," you know how to reframe your communication in a way that increases the possibility for understanding and agreement.

Being skillful interpersonally is also more than the mere application of the Golden Rule: Do unto others as you would have them do unto you. In terms of treating people with dignity and respect there is not a more important rule. A skill, however, requires that we go somewhat further: Do unto others as they want to be done unto. Simply put, others do not necessarily reason and have the same priorities as we do. They may be dedicated members of our team, but their commitment will be due to the fact that they feel their strengths and opinions are genuinely valued, and, as a result, they feel appreciated and acknowledged.

Becoming skillful requires practice. When we watch professional athletes hit a home run or put that golf ball inches from the hole, we are witnessing people who daily work on their swing until the rhythm and timing is automatic. No longer do they have to think consciously about every detail of what they are doing; the mechanics have been integrated into their behavior. Their focus now can be oriented primarily toward their goal.

WWhen you are not practicing, remember someone, somewhere, is practicing; and when you meet him, he will win.

Bill Bradley

To be skillful with people requires the same dedication. So if you consider yourself an "amateur" in this arena or feel a little "coaching" might be helpful, let me share with you a five-step process that, if practiced on a daily basis, will result in you being regarded as an "Interpersonal Skills Professional."

■ STEP ONE - BUILDING TRUST

All healthy human relationships, whether professional or personal, have as their foundation trust. If you trust someone, he or she has the potential to influence you. You have that same potential to influence those who trust you. But without trust, influence is almost impossible.

Nowhere is the importance of trust more evident than in the new world of work. Influence is clearly becoming less and less a function of position and more and more because of the ability to build **trust**. A person unwilling to take the time and effort to build trust in his or her professional and personal relationships will severely handicap his or her goal of being a thriver .

Creating an environment in which trust is dominant is being recognized as one of the most critical roles of the contemporary leader. Leaders today are starting to understand that although power may be attached to a title, an organization thrives when people are encouraged to use their own power. Effective leaders do not wield power, they empower. Rather than controlling people with bureaucratic systems and procedures, they free them up to create and innovate.

In other words, leaders are fast learning that although a paycheck may be a strong motivator to show up for work, it is being trusted, valued, and believed in that inspires people to cooperate and collaborate, which are core characteristics of a thriving organization.

After years of relative success as a leader, I decided to truly delegate those things others could do as well or better, doing mostly those things only I could do. Net results are significant growth of staff members' attitudes about self.

The biggest remaining problem is how team effort works. There is still much to do in helping others create a stronger synergy for the entire organization.

But I now have more time to focus on the big picture and to develop a compelling vision for the organization.

GENE BERGOFFEN – PRESIDENT AND CEO, NATIONAL PRIVATE TRUCK COUNCIL

In the magazine *For Executives Only,* Clarence Francis gives this advice: "You can buy a person's time; you can buy his physical presence in a given place; you can even buy a measured number of his skilled muscular motions per hour. But you cannot buy enthusiasm. You cannot buy initiative. You cannot buy the devotion of hearts, minds, and souls. You have to earn those things."

How do we earn a person's trust? First, by thinking about what builds trust and what destroys it.

Effective leaders do not control people with bureaucratic systems and procedures, they free them up to create and innovate.

David McNally

Consider for a moment some people you trust
and then complete the following exercise:

WHY DO YOU TRUST THEM?

HOW DO YOU FEEL ABOUT THEM?

HOW DO YOU RELATE TO THEM?

WHAT WOULD YOU DO FOR THEM?

Now let's see if you and I have anything in common with the people we trust. I trust them because their behavior has demonstrated, according to my values, that they are trustworthy. I feel positive toward them and tend to be more open with what I share about my personal and professional life. I enjoy being with them and would do whatever I could to be of assistance to them. I have confidence in and respect for them. As such, I give strong consideration to their views and advice. How do we compare?

Take some time now to assess honestly your feelings about the changes taking place in your workplace.

You can make your world so much larger
simply by acknowledging everyone else's.

JEANNE MARIE LASKAS

The
Eagle's
Secret

CAN YOU TRUST PEOPLE WHO LOOK DIFFERENT FROM YOU?

CAN YOU TRUST PEOPLE WHO ACT DIFFERENTLY FROM YOU?

CAN YOU TRUST PEOPLE WHO MAY SPEAK A DIFFERENT LANGUAGE FROM YOU?

DO YOU SEE NEW TYPES OF PEOPLE PROVIDING EXCITING BURSTS OF FRESH ENERGY?

OR

DO YOU RESIST COOPERATING WITH ANYONE WHO IS DIFFERENT FROM YOU?

To trust or not to trust is obviously a highly personal decision. Some people approach life with the attitude "I trust people when they prove it"; others reflect the opposite, "I trust people until they disprove it." In either case, as people cannot see our thoughts and intentions, their decision to trust or not to trust eventually is determined by our actions, our behavior.

ACTIONS BUILD OR DESTROY ➤ **TRUST**

Four specific behaviors do more to create trust than any others. Conversely, when these behaviors are lacking or not present in an individual, trust is diminished or destroyed. We will call them the elements of trust. As you read them, reflect on where you are strong and where there is room for improvement.

■ **RELIABILITY** - Do you do what you say you will do? Some people can get carried away with enthusiasm or can be overly anxious to please others. This can lead to making promises that are unable to be kept. Excuses may be accepted initially, but in the long run the word gets out: "likable but unreliable." Do you make promises that you often do not keep? Do you get carried away by the excitement of the moment, overcommit, and then have to let people down? Good intentions are important but, in the end, it is what you do that matters most.

F̶ool me once, shame on you,
fool me twice, shame on me.

Proverb

■ **STRAIGHTFORWARDNESS** - Does what you are saying line up with what you are thinking and feeling? Are you willing to challenge if you feel someone might be wrong? Some people are so concerned with others' feelings and conflict that they hold back or "fudge" when it comes to really saying how they feel. Being sensitive to others has merit, but not when other people feel that you are not being honest with them. It takes courage to be direct, but people then know, even if there is disagreement, that they are dealing with someone who will state where he or she stands on an issue.

■ **ACCEPTANCE** - Do you lack tolerance when others do not see your point of view? Do you judge others purely on the level of their professional competence? Do you get impatient when others seem to spend too much time getting to know each other? Efficiency has its place, but if people feel that their needs are not being considered or their different ways of doing things are not appreciated, trust is destroyed. People need to be recognized for their unique strengths and respected for their competencies. Behind every employee there is a person waiting to be acknowledged.

■ **OPENNESS** - Do you play your cards close to your chest? Do you freely share information, thoughts, and feelings? Are you someone who gives little feedback? Although akin to straightforwardness, openness is being willing to volunteer what might be helpful to the other person. Some people appear closed, which results in discomfort with people with whom they are communicating. Their unresolved question becomes: "Is there something more I could know that would help me?" It takes courage to be open, but the benefits are that free-flowing communication allows for more rapid solutions to problems and a more creative, stimulating environment.

Because every human being has natural strengths, you may quickly identify one or more elements as strong points for you. Honesty, however, usually has us uncertain about at least one element. That's okay, for to improve our trust-building ability requires that we know our starting point. Make a note now about what element of trust comes easily to you and, perhaps, which one you may need to examine.

I FEEL MY TRUST-BUILDING STRENGTH(S) IS (ARE):

A.

B.

THE ELEMENT(S) OF TRUST I NEED TO EXAMINE IS (ARE):

A.

B.

In the new world of work, both managers and employees share the responsibility to do whatever is possible to be regarded as trustworthy. Only where trust exists will people feel free to share ideas, accept feedback, tell the truth, and, most important, make a total commitment to create a thriving organization.

Nirmalya Kumar, professor of marketing at the International Institute for Management Development in Lausanne, Switzerland, who with the help of colleagues has been doing extensive research into the relative importance of trust in business, says: "What really distinguishes trusting from distrusting relationships is the ability of the parties to make a leap of faith: They believe that each is interested in the other's welfare and that neither will act without first considering the action's impact on the other."

As you reflect on your own capacity for trust building, consider the fact that you cannot change anybody. You can threaten or cajole, but, in the final analysis, change is a decision that comes from within the individual. You can, however, change yourself. And that is what being skillful interpersonally is all about, taking responsibility for your part for what is, or what is not, working in the relationship and being willing to change your own behavior to facilitate the building of trust.

The influence of each human being on others in this life is a kind of immortality.

John Quincy Adams

The
Eagle's
Secret

■ STEP TWO - SELF-AWARENESS

If it is our behavior that most affects a person's decision to trust or not to trust, an objective look at how others see us could greatly enhance our understanding of our effect on others, or, as we have all experienced, why some people take to us immediately while others are more cautious.

Learning about my own impact on others began with a behavioral model developed by Wilson Learning Corporation, an international consulting firm based in Minneapolis, Minnesota, with whom I've consulted for several years. The model divides people into four different personality types or social styles: **Amiable, Driver, Analytical,** and **Expressive**.

Within these groupings there are, admittedly, many individual differences, but, as a tool for getting closer to fully appreciating how others see us and why people think and behave the way they do, the model is quite powerful. As each style is described, examine yourself to see which one you most identify with.

■ **AMIABLE:** The two dominant behavioral influences of this style are that they combine informality with a mild or nonassertive approach to others. The result is a warm and open person. They are laid back when dealing with others and rarely show aggression. They are concerned with and care a great deal about people. Knowing what people are feeling and experiencing is very important to them. They are friendly and considerate, and listening is a natural ability. Their approach to life is to be cooperative and helpful. They dislike interpersonal conflict and can respond negatively to autocratic managers who they perceive as insensitive.

■ **DRIVER:** This style is the perceived opposite of the Amiable style. Their two dominant behavioral influences are formality combined with a more direct approach to others. The result is a take-charge, results-oriented person. Efficiency and thoroughness of execution are their priorities. They also are more autonomous and their work relationships tend to lean toward the value others bring to a situation. They are not afraid to confront if they disagree with others' opinions or conclusions. They may care about people but often see social interaction at work as an unproductive use of time.

■ **ANALYTICAL:** The two dominant behavioral influences of this style are that they combine formality with the Amiable style's milder or nonassertive approach to others. The results are observably reflective persons who think before they speak. They are not risk takers, preferring the company of those who they know well. They are more guarded with their emotions, keeping their feelings to themselves. They have a more deliberate, methodical approach to their daily lives. Precision and accuracy are their priorities and they like the time to make sure a job is done well. Because they give careful consideration and thought to a subject, they usually are very knowledgeable.

■ **EXPRESSIVE:** This style is the perceived opposite of the Analytical style. Their two dominant behavioral influences are informality combined with the Driver style's more direct approach to others. The results are spontaneous, outgoing people. They are often visibly bold and energetic and how they feel is obvious for they express their emotions freely. This does not mean that they are undisciplined, but they enjoy variety and situations that call for creativity and lots of people interaction. They are highly sociable and comfortable in public settings. Their enthusiasm is often contagious and, when not too effervescent, they are respected for their "natural" people skills.

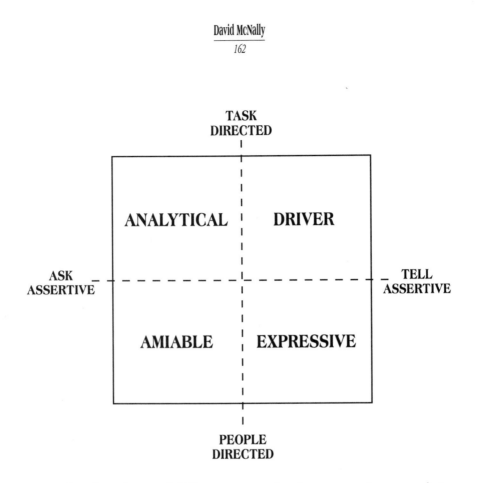

TASK
DIRECTED

ANALYTICAL | DRIVER

ASK
ASSERTIVE

TELL
ASSERTIVE

AMIABLE | EXPRESSIVE

PEOPLE
DIRECTED

So where do you fit? If you are experiencing some resistance to being "boxed in," that's understandable. Admittedly we are more complex creatures than the simple descriptions just presented. Social styles are broad brush-strokes, not detailed portraits. No one is exactly one style. Social style also is not a reflection of a person's drive, ambition, or intellectual capacity. You will find leaders in all of the styles and all of the styles in every profession or line of work.

Some people, however, obviously lean toward one style, while others are more difficult to define. You may be able to pick out people you know more easily than you can analyze yourself. A sense of humor also helps tremendously when playing with the model. A participant in one of my management seminars who had been identified by others who knew him well as definitely a Driver, but who "aggressively" resisted that categorization, came to the second day of the program and admitted reluctantly that his wife's response to the categorization was: "That's what I've been trying to tell you for twenty-five years."

How about your children or siblings? I certainly can pick out styles in mine, and it has changed the way I relate to them. Remember, the model is a learning tool; as such, it is meant to be constructive, not destructive. Avoid getting bogged down or defensive about the specifics of your individuality. Our objective is not to strip away your uniqueness but to take a leap forward in your awareness of how others see you and how they relate to you.

With this in mind, it is important to continue to expand our self-awareness by using the social-style model to understand the natural strengths and weaknesses of people when it comes to the elements of trust. Let's review each of the styles for this purpose.

Don't mistake personality for character.

Wilma Askinas

■ **AMIABLE:** What comes naturally to Amiable people is acceptance. Their strong people orientation makes them the least judgmental of all the styles. They want to like you and for you to like them. A cooperative and collaborative environment is their ideal. They build trust because they are genuinely interested in others. Straightforwardness, however, is not easy for this style for, to them, it puts the relationship at risk. They do not want to offend or hurt feelings. They need to learn that directness has its place when, for example, the success of a project is at stake and all points of view need to be heard and evaluated.

■ **DRIVER:** Being straightforward is a major asset of Drivers when it comes to trust building. Their efficient, results-oriented nature requires no-nonsense, "tell it to me straight" communication. Feelings are secondary to knowing the facts and opinions of others, to knowing exactly where a project or people are in terms of achieving set goals. You know where you stand with the driving style. They find accepting others a challenge because they tend to value people only for their contributions to the project or to the organization. Often they find taking time to discuss anything but the task to be accomplished very difficult. They need to learn that an investment in relationship building and getting to know people beyond what they "do" is an investment in success.

Nothing is so strong as gentleness,
and nothing is so gentle as real strength.

Ralph Stockman

■ **ANALYTICAL:** Because Analytical people give careful consideration before making commitments, they are known to be highly reliable. Their need to ensure that a project is completed with precision and even perfection, leads them to be cautious when asked for time lines and to set specific goals. This means that when Analytical people make an agreement they have often given considerable thought to the implications to ensure that they can keep the agreement. Their reserved, more private nature, however, can lead to a lack of openness when communicating with others. The fear of being wrong also can hold them back from offering opinions or information. They need to learn that open sharing of feelings and facts can be highly useful and productive in terms of building team spirit and stimulating creativity.

■ **EXPRESSIVE:** Openness is clearly the strength of the Expressive style when it comes to trust building. Such people love to know others on a personal level, and they want you to know others in the same way. When not carried to extreme, it gives them the mantle of being easy to like and fun to be around. They are people you feel you can "talk to" when you need a friendly ear. Because of their desire for recognition and to be well thought of, they can, however, promise too much. This can be compounded by the fact that their enthusiasm often leads to unrealistic expectations of what can be accomplished. They need to learn to pause and reflect before making promises because the power of their natural relationship-building ability is significantly diminished when others experience being "let down" after commitments are not met.

I**n matters of style, swim with the current.
In matters of principle, stand like a rock.**

Thomas Jefferson

The willingness to be fully aware of who we are and how we impact others, to be honest about our strengths and clear about our shortcomings, is a sign of a secure, confident person. Confidence is contagious. It has a powerful effect on others. People who both understand and are comfortable with themselves are more at ease when dealing with others. As such they tend to give more space to others' opinions and ideas. When people feel their intellects and skills are valued, their trust level skyrockets.

■ STEP THREE - PERCEPTIVENESS

When we are interacting with others, there is a strong tendency for us to be highly subjective, meaning we relate to them in terms of likes, dislikes, like me, unlike me, intelligent, a fool, and so on. Although this judgmental approach may be common, it is not helpful if we want truly to learn where others are "coming from." The same model we have used to define our own social style is equally as powerful in helping us move from being subjective to being objective and, as a result, more perceptive with others.

If you observe carefully, in other words, stay clearly focused whenever you are interacting with others, they will provide clues that help you identify their primary social style. Here are some additional characteristics of each of the four styles to help you become more perceptive.

The willingness to be honest about strengths and
clear about shortcomings is the sign of a secure, confident person.

David McNally

■ **AMIABLE:** Amiable people appear very approachable, for a smile often accompanies their greeting. They are attentive and usually wait for you to finish speaking before commenting or answering. They are most sensitive to your own level of comfort, and the way they feel often can be observed from responsive facial expressions showing whether they approve, disapprove, or feel happy or hurt. They tend to hold back in an aggressive environment, preferring to wait things out rather than jump into the fray. They like time to make decisions and resist "pushy" situations.

■ **DRIVER:** People with a driving style are assertive and enjoy taking charge of people and situations. They get down to business quickly and would prefer to avoid "small talk." Conversation or discussions with them can feel like arguments as they challenge and debate. It is a way, however, to consider all the options and to ensure all the right decisions are being made. They tend to withhold their feelings until they feel safe to express them. A fast-moving, results-oriented environment is their ideal.

■ **ANALYTICAL:** Analytical people appear quite formal and reserved. They are not unfriendly but they do tend to hold back in expressing both opinions and emotions. They ask questions rather than give directions because their purpose is to make sure that they have looked at a situation from every angle. They do not respond well to "undisciplined" environments where ideas are plentiful but where follow-through is negligible. Their insights and solutions come from careful examination of the facts and attention to detail.

■ **EXPRESSIVE:** Expressive people readily shake your hand and introduce you to others. They are spontaneous and demonstrative with opinions and feelings. They may even interrupt or be impatient with what they perceive to be slow-moving conversation or lack of action. They rely strongly on their "gut" and intuition when making decisions. A creative, action-oriented environment is the one that brings out their multiple ideas for solving problems and achieving goals. They are recognizable for their good humor.

John Richards, an accountant in a large corporation, learned the value of perceptiveness when he was assigned with six other employees to a new business start-up team. Right off the bat, he hated the assignment. "I've already got too much to do," he complained. "I hate meeting early because I'm just not a morning person." If it hadn't been for a perceptive team leader, John's attitude could have sunk the team. "Helen understood social styles," John said, after the team had completed its mission successfully. "She complemented us on having different styles and helped us understand that our strength was in our various educational backgrounds, problem-solving skills, points of view, work paces, moods, and demeanors. To me this was a powerful concept, and it worked."

Understanding social styles is a powerful concept not only because it is simple and accessible but precisely, as John Richards discovered, because it does work!

There is only one thing about which I'm certain, there is very little about which one can be certain.

SOMERSET MAUGHAM

Two years ago I had a vision for a technology plan for our school district. Budgets were tight, departments fought over every dollar to purchase new technology, and there was a real division between the academic and business sides of the district.

I went to my boss who said, "Go ahead but there will not be any money," and "are you sure you want to open this can of worms?" He suggested that I present the idea to the superintendent and see if the plan could become a "priority" in our district improvement plan for the next year. I represent the business side of the district, so I spoke with my counterpart on the academic side. She liked the idea too.

We co-chaired a committee for almost two years and created a fifteen-page written plan for technology. We presented it to the cabinet, school board, and public. Everyone was supportive but with no way to raise the $33 million.

To make a long story short, the cabinet somehow came up with $4 million to begin the implementation process this next year.

I believe with the right attitude, the players, and the right idea, you can make anything happen.

JIM VILLARS – INFORMATION SYSTEMS COORDINATOR, EDUCATION (K-12)

The right attitudes, the right players, and the right ideas can come together for all of us when we make a commitment to practicing interpersonal skills. This happens when we take all that we have learned so far in steps 1, 2, and 3 and apply that knowledge in step 4.

■ STEP FOUR - VERSATILITY

Versatility is the ability to understand and work in the "world" of another. It means valuing differences so we look for a person's strengths not weaknesses. It means respecting different ways of learning, hearing, and processing information. Here are some characteristics of a versatile person:

- Win/Win-oriented

- Adaptable

- Situational

- Can express or withhold feelings as appropriate

- Can talk or listen as needed

- Values others

- Negotiable

- Responsive

- Resilient

- Considerate

Of course, we run the risk here of describing what some might call the "perfect" person. That is not the intent. But we do need to know what versatility means and, if others would use some of the above words to describe us, then we know that being truly skillful with people is within our grasp.

Let's take another look at the four social styles to increase our knowledge of what it means to be versatile and move into another's "world."

■ **AMIABLE:** To work effectively with Amiable people allow time to build a personal relationship, be attentive to their concerns, and move at an easier pace with discussions and negotiations. They like harmony and are committed team players. They are also very loyal to those whom they feel genuinely care about them. If presenting or discussing an idea, consider the effects what is being talked about has on people. Look for benefits that demonstrate how people will be helped, their jobs will be less stressful, they will have greater support or perhaps a more stable environment. Amiable people understand the importance of the bottom line, but it is your sensitivity to the "people issues" that will win their commitment.

■ **DRIVER:** To work effectively with Drivers, respect their time and be well prepared. Be straightforward and confident in your views. Leave personal questions out of discussions unless invited because Drivers tend to be private about their personal lives. They enjoy the respect that comes from achievements. If presenting or discussing an idea, focus on how much more will be accomplished because of its implementation. Stress improvements in productivity, quality, and more efficient use of resources. Drivers understand that people make things happen, but it is the "bottom line" that makes jobs, wages, and growth possible.

Speak the truth,
but leave immediately after.

Slovenian Proverb

■ **ANALYTICAL:** To work effectively with Analytical people, be willing to answer many questions and provide numerous details. Give as much time as possible for a response to a question or a task to be completed. This ensures that Analytical people's need to process and think through an answer is respected. They are more quiet in social situations but can have a good sense of humor. They respond well to those whom they see as being thoughtful and rational. When presenting or discussing an idea, have facts, figures, and evidence accessible to prove your conclusions. Focus on benefits of greater safety, elimination or reduction of mistakes, or more security.

■ **EXPRESSIVE:** To work effectively with Expressive people, be open and willing to listen to their thoughts and feelings. Personal relationships are very important to them, so invest time getting to know who they are. They like to think that they know you so "shooting the breeze" is not necessarily a waste of time for them. If presenting or discussing an idea, focus on how this will eliminate a lot of finicky, mundane work that saps their energy and holds them up from moving on to more exciting new challenges. Describe the big picture benefits and avoid "boring" details. But be ready for some insightful, provocative questions.

At Quaker Oats' breakfast division versatility is firmly embedded in the culture. From initial concept development through prototype development and qualitative research, food scientists and engineers work closely with marketing and marketing research to create, test, and refine the company's cereals and other breakfast foods to develop a formula that can hold its own and compete on the intensely competitive grocery store shelves.

As vice president Polly Kawalek explains, "The retail customer is looking for something that's going to help him sell more groceries. He's not interested in something that would be good for Quaker. That's why everybody across the whole team gets involved in product development. You have to engineer a package that will protect the product through transport and handling en route to the point of sale."

Versatility is what makes this Quaker group a team not only in name but in cooperation, support, and appreciation for the value of each other's contribution.

Being versatile with people does not mean sacrificing our own personality or way of doing things. Rather it means we are willing to look at another view, we are not intractable or unyielding, we are open to negotiation, and we make the effort to explain things in terms that others value and understand.

Now might be a good time to assess your relationships with the people in your workplace. Remember, only with practice can you become an Interpersonal Skills Professional. Take some time to work on your versatility by completing the following exercise. As you answer the questions, you will learn how you perceive fellow employees and customers who are "different" from you. Based on this self-examination, you then can formulate with each of them action steps to build trust.

When people are treated with dignity and given a chance to speak in their own way, barriers can be broken down, if not overcome.

JOHN FRANCIS BURKE

■ CULTIVATING YOUR GARDEN OF DIFFERENCES

In the left-hand column, make a list of fellow employees or customers you interact with. Include people you interact with everyday, people you interact with now and then, and people you rarely see.

In the second column, indicate how you are alike.

In the third column, indicate any "Communication Challenges" that exist between you and each person you have listed. How is this person different from you? It may be as elementary as this: You are a man and the other person is a woman. Maybe the person has more authority than you do. Or maybe the person is from a different culture.

In the last column, list steps you can take to increase trust between yourself and that person. Whenever people are in any form of conflict, the issue is almost always trust or, more specifically, lack of trust. When you actually write down differences as you perceive them, then you can address practical ways you can build trust. Your efforts in this regard will pay enormous dividends.

You never really understand a person
until you consider things from his point of view.

HARPER LEE

CULTIVATING YOUR GARDEN OF DIFFERENCES: BUILDING TRUST

PEOPLE I INTERACT WITH	SIMILARITIES	COMMUNICATION CHALLENGES	STEPS TO BUILDING TRUST
DAILY			
PERIODICALLY			
RARELY			

Your versatility, in other words your respect and appreciation for the way others work best, will result in a more positive and favorable reaction to you. Problems will be resolved more quickly, cooperation and teamwork will improve, and work will get done more efficiently. In the landmark book *Valuing Diversity,* editors Lewis Brown Griggs and Lente-Louise Louw state: "The relationship process with its potential for creativity is the lifeblood of every organization. In this world in which challenge and change are the only constants, effective personal, interpersonal, and organizational relationships are the most critical tools available for our survival and the vehicles for our success."

What gives a team richness, texture, and, ultimately, resourcefulness is the uniqueness of its members and an artful linking of their diverse gifts.

Allan Cox

■ STEP FIVE - ATTITUDE

So far in this chapter we have dealt with the "why to" and "how to" of developing interpersonal skills. None of this has any consequence, however, unless we also "want to" understand and effectively relate to those who are different from us. The "want to" is a reflection of our attitude, and there is no aspect of our lives where attitude does not play the major role in the outcome.

In an article in *Fast Company* magazine, Peter Carbonara says that "Hire for Attitude - Train for Skill" has become the new mantra as many companies have begun to realize that you can't build a great company without great people. In their quest to hire the "right" people for their organizations, they have come to the conclusion that "what people know is less important than who they are." A major part of who they are includes respect for their coworkers, personal flexibility, and a willingness to be a committed team player.

Here are some suggestions on how to develop the "want to" attitude:

■ **WALK IN SOMEONE ELSE'S SHOES.** You may be faced with coworkers who have physical disabilities. Take the time to get to know some of them. Let them share with you the challenges they face that able-bodied people rarely think about. Learn the depth of their feelings on the issues you also care about. Experience their commitment to doing great work. It will give you a rare insight into what it's like to negotiate barriers that you may never have thought existed.

Yearn to understand first and to be understood second.

Beca Lewis Allen

■ **SHARE A MEAL.** Where I live breakfast meetings are big. They're tough if you're not a morning person, but they are great opportunities to develop relationships with people at work and to cultivate your professional network of contacts. Lunchtime is another opportunity to get out and visit with customers, attend professional association meetings, company-sponsored brown bag seminars, and other group meetings where you can develop business relationships on a more personal level.

■ **RESPECT CUSTOMER CULTURE.** Strive to understand and respect your customers' language, values, and traditions. Recognize that even the buildings you erect can attract or repel people of different cultures. Realizing that the Chinese community appreciates architecture that conforms to their ideals of harmony with the elements in nature, one company changed the lighting in a building when they realized that Chinese associated the blue-light tinge with death.

■ **COMMUNICATE.** In your office, you might notice that one person on your team rarely takes the initiative in a discussion or doesn't make eye contact with you. Instead of assuming the person is a pushover or doesn't like you, dig a little deeper. You may find that this person simply is shy or comes from a culture where people are expected to defer to those in authority.

■ **VOLUNTEER.** Serve on a task force, committee, or board that is dealing with an issue that you care about. In the process of working together, you may gain a deeper appreciation for the power of teamwork and how much can be accomplished. It's a powerful experience that, when transferred, will enhance the quality of your personal and professional relationships.

■ **PARTICIPATE.** Sign up for an experiential or outdoor learning experience. Some of the most powerful learning about group dynamics occurs when people are taken out of their normal day-to-day routines and offered unusual or unique opportunities to break through personal limitations in thought or behavior. In the supportive atmosphere of an experiential learning workshop, participants gain new insights into how their own behaviors and attitudes toward others may be holding them back.

■ **LISTEN.** Successful interaction with almost anyone is no more complex than being genuinely interested in him or her. And it is your willingness to truly listen that validates that interest. In fact, more understanding, more appreciation, more camaraderie, more teamwork, more affection, more love, more cooperation, and more laughter have ensued from the simple act of listening than from any words ever spoken by the world's greatest orators.

Our attitudes, the approach we bring to life, are the seeds with which we create our lives. The more we wish to experience love, harmony, support, encouragement, and recognition in our lives, the more we need to express those qualities to others. This is not wishy-washy, touchy-feely stuff, this is the greatest "stuff" in the world. Human beings get a significant portion of their self-worth from successful interaction with others. Affiliation, acknowledgment, affection, and affirmation nourish our humanity, and feed our souls.

I note the obvious differences
in the human family.
Some of us are serious,
Some thrive on comedy …

The variety of our skin tones
can confuse, bemuse, delight,
brown and pink and beige and purple,
tan and blue and white.

I've sailed upon the seven seas
and stopped in every land.
I've seen the wonders of the world,
not yet one common man.

I know ten thousand women
called Jane and Mary Jane,
but I've not seen any two
who really were the same …

I note the obvious differences
between each sort and type,
but we are more alike, my friends,
than we are unalike.

We are more alike, my friends,
than we are unalike …

EXCERPTS FROM "THE HUMAN FAMILY"
BY MAYA ANGELOU

The
Eagle's
Secret

SURVIVORS FOCUS ON	THRIVERS FOCUS ON
■ Hanging In	■ Hanging Out
■ Personal Perceptions	■ Making Connections
■ Working With Others	■ Working With Teammates
■ Differences As A Problem	■ Differences As A Solution
■ Desiring Conformity	■ Valuing Diversity
■ What Is Tried And True	■ What Is True And Untried

HOW TO CREATE A THRIVING ORGANIZATION

- ■ Lead by example
- ■ Build a culture of trust
- ■ Understand the purpose of leadership – to empower, to free up, and to serve
- ■ Remember, solutions reside in the brains of people
- ■ Delegate authority
- ■ Remove bureaucracy

- ■ Solicit ideas from everyone
- ■ Provide forums for honest dialogue
- ■ Identify values and stick to them, unless something more inspiring comes along
- ■ Keep everyone informed as to how they are doing regarding their goals and the goals of the organization

7

Nourishing Heart, Mind & Soul

Three-Part Harmony

Thrivers know what matters —
they seek performance with fulfillment.

From the time I was fifteen until I was twenty-four, I spent most of my weekends, vacations, and "sick" days from work surfing the beaches of my home state of South Australia. I was not a particularly good surfer, but I loved it with a passion. As my children now poke good-natured fun at my soft waistline and expanding bald spot, they find it hard to believe that the guy in the photos with the deep tan, blond hair, and muscles is their father. In my defense, they also find it difficult to believe that the girl by his side in the tiny bikini is their mother. But I swear it is us!

There is no thrill like riding the perfect wave. No roller coaster has yet been invented that can compete with the magnificence and power of the ocean. To combine with this force of nature and experience harmony with its flow is awesome in the truest sense of the word.

In their best-selling book, *If it ain't broke...BREAK IT!*, authors Robert Kriegel and Louis Patler offer the "Surfers' Rules." Now perhaps, like me, your days of risking life and limb at that level are over, and so finding the perfect wave is not on your list of goals. Nonetheless, these "rules" could easily be the philosophy of any thriver.

Here they are:

- **Passion Rules**
- **No Dare, No Flair**
- **Expect To Wipe Out**
- **Never Turn Your Back On The Ocean**
- **Keep Looking "Outside" For The Next Opportunity**
- **Move Before It Moves You**
- **Never Surf Alone**

The authors sum up the importance of applying the rules by stating: "The future is coming towards us like enormous waves of change. The surf is up from California to Calgary to Calcutta. But how we respond is a matter of choice. We can stay on the beach or get out into the water."

In the surfing world there are individuals called "posers." These people hang around, dressed in all the right gear, but never actually get in among the waves. The thrill, the experience of surfing will never be theirs. Some people "pose" as thrivers. If posing as a thriver is not what we are about, then we must have the integrity to distinguish the feeling, the thrill of thriving, from the appearance of thriving. In other words, what a hollow victory it would be if, to the world, it appears we are thriving, but our inner experience is something radically different.

One of the best of all
earthly possessions is self-possession.

George D. Prentice

In the preface to this book I defined thriving as growing and prospering. The **experience** of thriving, therefore, is humankind's ultimate quest: a **rich external and internal life**. How do we create that?

There are two deeply felt trends in developed societies today. One is the ongoing necessity of improving the quality of our products and services if we are to compete effectively in a global economy. Another, equally as pressing and evident, is the desire by large sections of the population to improve the quality of their lives. These trends, if viewed in isolation, have the potential to cause great disharmony, for each demands a strong commitment.

"Keep your life in balance" is the advice commonly offered to those caught trying to "juggle" what often are viewed as competing responsibilities and obligations. Juggling? Balancing? These words evoke visuals of keeping a number of balls up in the air at the same time or walking a tightrope without a safety net. Doing this might be fun for the circus performer, but for the rest of us each undoubtedly causes considerable stress and tension. Although one of my clients did confront me recently with: "Our lives are like a circus! Why do you think these Dilbert cartoons are pinned up everywhere?"

Is there a solution, or are we doomed forever to be out of equilibrium?

If we accept that the pressures of competition and new technologies demand that organizations be in a constant state of transformation and that change will be an integral part of our daily lives, then to meet the standards we desire for both our work and our personal lives, we need a word that accurately defines what we wish to accomplish.

The word "blend" means: to merge, to combine harmoniously, to bring together seamlessly. Is this not a more accurate description of our desires? If we could orchestrate our "to do" lists in such a way that at the end of the day we feel fulfilled rather than frustrated, would finding out how to do so not be worthy of the deepest commitment?

You might not have considered, however, what this will require, **courage.** It is easy to give lip service to the desire for greater harmony in our lives, for, in this uncertain work world, the demands of those who employ us cannot be ignored. Even the best of intentions can dissolve quickly when faced with choosing between keeping a promise to attend a kid's ball game or responding to a last-minute request to stay late and finish a project. While completing the project is an understandable response to an unforgiving marketplace, the conflict might be that we're running out of ball games!

To have courage is to act as one believes one should.

Whenever we choose to live according to our values, we are courageous. Whenever we risk criticism from others by taking a stand on our beliefs, we are courageous. Whenever we define success in our own terms and work toward it, we are courageous. Whenever we admit to mistakes and apologize, we are courageous. Whenever we forgive others for their mistakes, we are courageous. Whenever we totally commit ourselves, we are courageous. Whenever we express gratitude for life itself, we are courageous. Whenever we face adversity yet still "show up" to meet our responsibilities, we are courageous.

When I have to, I work furiously because I am furious that I have to work.

George Soros

You are courageous. It takes courage to read a book like this. You are not hiding out, ignoring what you want from life, blaming others for your circumstances, unwilling to change. You would not have gotten this far unless you had demonstrated your courage by reading, reflecting, considering, arguing, disagreeing, accepting, questioning, answering, and challenging. You are doing this because you have the courage to ask from life all that it has to offer. You have the courage to be a thriver!

I have a coworker who chose to leave the workforce and stay home to be an influence on her two sons. When they entered high school, she went back to school and finished her undergraduate work. Since reentering the work world, she has used the skills she developed in managing a household and being a nurturing parent to become a cost-conscious, nurturing supervisor.

She has also continued to educate herself. She has earned an MBA and is a candidate for professional certification as an internal auditor. She is open-minded but focused, tough but nurturing, cost-conscious but not cheap. I have no doubt that she will be promoted to manager in the next two to three years.

GLEN YOUNG – INTERNAL AUDITOR,
CENTRAL & SOUTHWEST SERVICES

In this next stage of our journey toward thriving, our objective is to learn how to move from the unsettling juggling of our personal and professional lives to a more seamless "blending" of them together. In other words, rather than responding to them as competing forces, we understand that both are important and worthy of commitment and that both require attention if we are to be happy. It is now a matter of discovering how to clarify priorities so that a greater harmony results.

At the beginning of any change or when creating something new, it is always wise to assess present reality. Take a few moments now to kick back and reflect on where life currently has brought you.

Imagine yourself an eagle soaring above time and space. Below is the vast expanse of your life. You spread your wings and glide above the peaks and valleys, surveying the personal and professional decisions you've made, the actions taken, the joys and sorrows experienced.

The major forces and influences in your life, career, family, relationships, friends, experiences, appear as rivers. At certain points two or more rivers flow together, becoming forces of vast importance in your life: marriage, birth, leaving or maybe losing loved ones.

You pull in your wings slightly and drift downward. Your vision is pulled toward a river that is deep, wide, and powerful. Into its waters three other major rivers ultimately flow. As you gaze at this river, you recognize it as the reflection of your highest or best self.

Your best self is the harmonious blending of three dynamic and interactive elements: your soul, your heart, and your creative mind. Through our souls we express ourselves spiritually, through our hearts we express ourselves emotionally, and through our minds we express ourselves creatively. When we nourish these three aspects of our lives, the rewards are powerful.

Money ain't everything, but poverty ain't either.

W. ROYSTER

The
Eagle's
Secret

We see greater possibilities for our own lives and those of our families. We are more flexible and resilient. We are more adaptable, more willing and able to handle change. We are much more focused and positive in all that we do.

Failing to attend to our higher selves turns us into limited, less fulfilled human beings. Ultimately it hinders our ability to fully appreciate our achievements.

I personally have had to make some changes in my life. Last August I totally burned out. I couldn't function, couldn't concentrate, and cried at the drop of a hat. This was so unlike anything I had ever experienced.

I worked with a counselor of our Employee Assistance program and was referred to another. I took one month off (still wasn't enough!), but prioritized my life with "Me as Number One." I had forgotten to do that, even though I am in a helping profession and talk about it with others.

I learned a lot about myself in that one month, where my negative thinking came from and what changes I needed to make. With support from my counseling, I'm learning to look at what's important and what's not, saying "no," delegating, and creating a less stressful atmosphere.

It is not a comfortable pattern yet and it may never be, but I keep telling myself that I cannot ever go back to how I felt last fall.

SANDY MANDERFELD – VOLUNTEER COORDINATOR , ST. CLOUD HOSPITAL

**There cannot be a crisis until next week.
My schedule is already full.**

Henry Kissinger

Our best self, however, should not be separated from how we earn a living, any more than it cannot be separated from any other important aspect of our lives. When we try to create such a separation, we make ourselves less effective, both on and off the job. As management consultant Stephen Boehlke puts it, "I've had more than one senior executive tell me, 'When I come to work, I check my best self at the door.' And when I talk in training sessions about bringing the whole self to work, people sometimes say 'Why should I?' But the ultimate result of such an attitude is an inability to trust our inner selves."

Thrivers are constantly reevaluating their needs, values, and priorities. They recognize that values and priorities change over time and so make appropriate course corrections to compensate. They also see how all of their experiences are valuable and contribute to wholeness in their lives. Because each of us is unique, there is no one-size-fits-all prescription for attending to the needs of your own mind, heart, and soul.

The following process will help you discover what activities address those needs.

When you're finished, examine your lists thoroughly. If any activity seems impossible, an unrealistic fantasy, see if you can find a way to modify it to the point where it might become a possibility, if not now, then sometime in the future.

As you reflect on where you are and where you want to be, give
yourself adequate time to fully answer each of the following questions.
Write down everything that comes to mind, no matter how absurd or
unrealistic it may appear to be. Avoid censoring yourself for any reason.
Include activities that strike you as fun or lighthearted.

WHAT FULFILLS ME?

WHAT INSPIRES ME?

WHO INSPIRES ME?

WHAT DELIGHTS ME?

WHAT DO I VALUE?

WHOM DO I VALUE?

WHAT DO I FEEL CALLED TO DO?

Now move from reflection to action, for it is action that alters our experience. Look at your first set of lists for a moment for they will be the basis of your answers to the next three questions.

WHAT CAN I START DOING TODAY TO MAKE MY LIFE MORE MEANINGFUL?

WHAT WILL I BEGIN DOING WITHIN THE NEXT THIRTY DAYS
TO BRING A GREATER SENSE OF SATISFACTION TO MY LIFE?

WHAT WILL I DO WITHIN THE NEXT YEAR
TO TRANSFORM MY DREAMS INTO REALITY?

The items on these three new lists should be those to which you wish to give priority. They should reflect what fulfills and makes a difference to you. And each list has its own timetable for introducing the items on it into your life. Your next step is to start actually doing some or all of these activities by building them into your schedule on a regular basis.

Whatever is important to you: time to meditate, time to think, time to watch cartoons with your kids or nap with your spouse, then honor that activity by giving it a place on your schedule. And don't think of time for yourself as "overflow time" that can be reassigned to other activities when things run longer than you expect. Instead think of it as "inflow" time, those creative moments when good ideas or great thoughts emerge to inspire and encourage.

Honoring your best self is the most rewarding experience that life has to offer. It is also a lasting legacy to future generations, a contribution that will multiply and grow in a thousand positive ways.

But let's recognize that what we are discussing, although appealing and attractive, is not easy to implement. In *Catholic Digest* magazine, Bette Howland commented: "For a long time it seemed to me that life was about to begin, but there was always some obstacle in the way. Something had to be got through first, some unfinished business; time still to be served, a debt to be paid. Then life would begin. At last it dawned on me that these obstacles were my life."

If you identify with Bette, here is another practical way to put the ideas we have been discussing into action.

Reality says that very rarely does a busy person complete everything on his or her "to do" on any single day. That is why companies have earned fortunes helping people to prioritize. How do we ensure then that in our highly organized "doing," we are "being" the person we want to be? Only by clarifying on a daily basis what truly matters to us and then making a commitment to those items being accomplished. The following three questions will help you do that.

If we only stop trying to be happy we'd have a pretty good time.

EDITH WHARTON

**WHAT IS ONE CONCRETE, PRACTICAL THING I CAN DO TODAY
TO IMPROVE MYSELF PROFESSIONALLY?**

**WHAT IS ONE CONCRETE, PRACTICAL THING I CAN DO TODAY
TO IMPROVE THE QUALITY OF MY LIFE?**

**WHAT IS ONE CONCRETE, PRACTICAL THING I CAN DO TODAY
TO IMPROVE THE QUALITY OF OTHER PEOPLE'S LIVES?**

Write your answers in your daily planner or any other notebook that helps you to remember them. As you go through your day, give priority to each of these small, or not so small, goals. If you do this each day for a single year, you will have improved both your own life and that of others almost 1,100 times.

When you arrange your time in this way so that you honor your best self, your life gets better because you are doing daily those things that make it better. At first it may sound as if committing to these items will restrict your time. But, paradoxically, the reality is the opposite. Allocating the time to accomplish what you feel truly matters means that you are choosing freedom, to keep control in the face of the same pressures, the very same circumstances that force many people to feel out of control.

Every evening I turn my worries over to God.
He's going to be up all night anyway.

Mary C. Crowley

The
Eagle's
Secret

Time is the most precious of all commodities. There is wisdom in recognizing that you can't do it all. You must ask then what is truly important.

At the core of my personal mission statement is "to transform lives." There is a sense of integration when you put something noble (bigger than yourself) at the center of your life.

Enabling and empowering others is both the means and the end in what I am doing with my life as I endeavor to blend my roles as father, husband, CEO, and leader in my industry. For my roles within these roles are predominantly that of teacher, mentor, and coach.

I don't claim to be particularly good at enabling and empowering, but it is something I have identified that fulfills me.

I may always have the push and pull of daily life, but staying true to my mission allows for greater harmony.

JAMES GABBERT – CEO, GABBERTS INC.
NATIONAL FURNITURE RETAILER

The joy of life is made up of seemingly mundane victories
that give us our own small satisfactions.

BILLY JOEL

The
Eagle's
Secret

We cannot complete this chapter without giving serious consideration to that which goes beyond prioritizing our constantly changing commitments. Although we may graduate into an admirable practitioner of blending our daily activities to reflect what we value and believe in, each of us needs to break away for a more extensive time to rediscover who we are apart from the tasks we perform and the promises we make.

Again, this is not easy. "The place would fall apart without me!" "My desk would be impossible when I returned!" "Right now it would be too selfish to be away!" These are but a few of the reasons people give for not taking more than a few days off from work. In fact, the average length of a vacation for an American worker actually has diminished to three days. It's not that people aren't allocated longer vacations, they're just concerned about being away from their jobs for a longer time. But does this short-term focus serve or hinder our long-term growth?

In Australia, where I grew up, people routinely take their full three- to four-week vacations with glee, and in France, virtually the whole country takes off the month of August every year. In one of my audiences a short time back, there were a number of delegates from France. I asked them if what I have just related to you is true. "Yes," they replied. "But we also spend July preparing for August."

The sun will set without thy assistance.

THE TALMUD

Those of us who are "indispensable" are faced once more with the need for courage. Three days is not a "vacation." It's not long enough for us to vacate our thoughts about work or the physical rhythms of our busy schedules. We need adequate time to depart fully from our regular obligations and normal day-to-day routines. We need to step completely outside of our habitual world so that we can wind down and rest. We need renewal and rejuvenation.

We also need to remind ourselves that the new world of work demands creative, contributing, committed human beings. Only those who "invest" the time to re-create themselves physically, spiritually, mentally, and emotionally will be able to meet those requirements.

Spend each day as if it were your last...
and you will be broke by sunset.

Los Angeles Times Syndicate

The
Eagle's
Secret

What else can you do to make your life fuller, more rewarding, and more nourishing? Here are a few suggestions:

■ **LIGHTEN UP.** I recently interviewed an executive of one of the world's largest financial services companies. He surprised me by saying very early in our conversation that a characteristic he believed was essential for thriving in the new world of work was the ability to have fun and laugh. He suggested that a sense of humor was an excellent sign of good self-esteem and a healthy perspective.

Humor is a now a medically proven safety valve. It helps to free us for a moment from the stresses and pressures of life. In the course of a single day, a well-developed sense of humor can provide a dozen or more very brief "vacations" from the forces and people we find difficult to handle. We must learn that we can take things seriously without being solemn. We must become capable of laughing rather than chafing at human foibles and foul-ups, including our own.

■ **DESIGN SOMETHING.** Are you unhappy with the way your work space is set up? Sketch out some ways of rearranging it that might be more practical, efficient, or comfortable. Wish you had a chart that would show exactly how each division of your company supports its organizational mission? Draw one up yourself. Often this kind of "wishful visualization" leads to some very worthwhile ideas, many of which can be translated into specific improvements or valuable additions. But even if your ideas never get off the drawing board, thinking like this helps to keep your mind sharp and your creativity flowing.

If I could drop dead right now, I'd be the happiest man alive.

Samuel Goldwyn

■ **INVENT SOMETHING.** Instead of just wishing for a better mousetrap, or office chair, or pasta sauce, or method for teaching kids math, spend some time creating it yourself. Depending on your skills, you might simply write up your ideas, or draw diagrams, or build a working prototype, or devise an entire system. Developing these ideas can unleash vast creative forces inside you. And if your invention is a worthy one, it also could lead to a promotion, more money, and perhaps even a whole new direction in your life.

■ **KEEP A JOURNAL.** This can be a personal diary; a book of your own insights, reflections, and observations; a record of others' ideas and affirmations that are meaningful to you; or a place to write essays, poems, or stories of your own. Some people set aside regular times to write in their journals; others carry their journals with them, some as a file on their laptop computers, and write in them when they feel it is important to do so.

■ **MEDITATE.** Although meditation is a highly effective stress reducer and relaxation technique, it is also a powerful tool for focusing, for enhancing creativity, and for promoting clarity and insight. Meditation comes in a variety of styles and methods, some secular, some religious. Some styles are costly to learn, but most are free or inexpensive. Design your own style of meditation.

Looking back, I was always writing. Twaddle it was too. But far better write twaddle than nothing at all.

Katherine Mansfield

■ **CREATE A WORK OF ART.** Drawing, woodworking, writing, playing music, painting, sculpting, and acting all can put you more in touch with your higher self, and are pleasurable at the same time. If you're an absolute beginner, take an introductory class through a community center or college extension program. Or, teach yourself through trial and error.

■ **EXERCISE.** Light to moderate exercise helps to reduce stress and make us more flexible physically, mentally, and emotionally. Many of the world's greatest thinkers and leaders regularly take long walks, usually alone. Walking focuses their thoughts, and helps them to center themselves. Some say that they get their very best ideas while walking. I walk three miles early each morning immediately after I wake up. I use the time to brush away the mental cobwebs, affirm what I want for my life, and reflect on what I want to accomplish during the day. I find these walks grounding, energizing, and relaxing.

■ **SLEEP MORE.** Our commonly held view is that sleep is unproductive, a waste of time. But studies have shown that too little sleep makes people into less effective performers and thinkers. The getting of enough sleep literally can make you sharper, more focused, and more effective at what you do. Many highly successful people regularly take afternoon naps, and in many countries, such as Italy, Spain, and Mexico, "siesta" is the norm.

■ **TAKE TIME TO THINK AND REFLECT.** Most of us have become so action oriented, that we don't put aside time to consider what it all means, who we are, and where we are headed. In contrast, many successful people tell me that their most productive time of all, the time when they get their best ideas and biggest insights, is when they close their door and allow themselves to contemplate and ponder.

Finally I would like to recommend an exercise with which to complete your day. It is the acknowledgment of someone you may rarely acknowledge: yourself!

Each night, as you get ready for bed, or just before you turn out the light, spend a couple of moments asking yourself the following questions:

What did I learn today?

What did I do today to improve the quality of my work?

What did I do today to make my life more meaningful?

These questions achieve two objectives. They are a way to pat yourself on the back and to keep your life on track. Keep in mind that perfection is not the goal, it is progress. It is the continual movement toward the rich internal and external life that we described earlier as the **experience** of thriving.

Laughter is wine for the soul.

Once we can laugh, we can live.

It is the hilarious declaration by man that life is worth living.

Man is always hopeful of, always pushing towards better things.

Laughter is brought in to mock at things

as they are so that they may topple down,

and make room for better things to come.

SEAN O'CASEY

SURVIVORS **FOCUS ON**	**THRIVERS** **FOCUS ON**
▪ Putting Out Fires	▪ Blazing A Trail
▪ Being Cautious	▪ Being Courageous
▪ What's Safe	▪ What's True
▪ What I Can Get	▪ What I Can Give
▪ The Obstacle	▪ The Dream
▪ The Future As Uncertain	▪ The Future As Unlimited

HOW TO CREATE A THRIVING ORGANIZATION

- Lead by example
- Be sensitive to overload and burnout
- Develop high ethical standards and commit to them
- Respect the need for mental, physical, and spiritual renewal
- Plan for unexpected intrusions on employees' personal lives
- Encourage vacations
- Provide opportunities for social interaction between employees
- Create a sense of community
- Treat employees in the way you would have them treat their customers

8

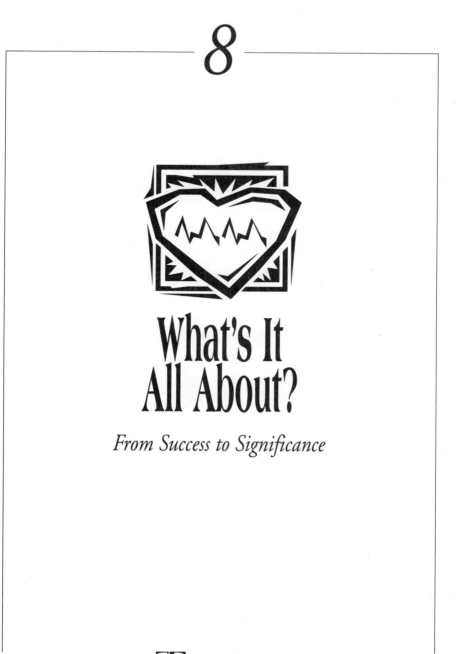

What's It All About?

From Success to Significance

Thrivers love life —
they accept joy and pain as part of the game.

AT THE AGE OF EIGHTY-NINE, at a time when many people are barely hanging on or are already dead, lifelong explorer and adventurer Norman Vaughan was still striving to reach his peak. In January 1995 Vaughan spent eight days struggling against 40-knot gusts of wind and arctic cold to become the first person to scale the 10,302-foot mountain that he and legendary explorer Richard Byrd had discovered on an expedition some sixty-five years earlier. After several previous attempts, Vaughan and his team finally reached the summit of Mt. Vaughan just three days shy of his eighty-ninth birthday.

At a news conference following the climb, this former car salesman, snowmobile racer, and ski instructor informed reporters that he would have made the trip more quickly if a fused right ankle and knee replacement hadn't forced him to climb straight up the mountain. Asked to reflect on the lessons of his latest achievement and his long life, he told a *Washington Post* reporter that achieving lofty goals and having great adventures are not important for what they can get you externally; what really matters is the challenge, confidence, and self-discovery that they provide people on the inside.

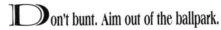

Don't bunt. Aim out of the ballpark.

David Ogilvy

"You don't hear so much about people with a dream today," Vaughan said. "It's almost as if they're afraid to discover what they're individually capable of and would rather just follow the other fellow. But all of us have more inside us than we believe possible. We have to dream big and dare to fail to bring it out."

Janis Hahn was seventeen and in the hospital being treated for cancer. But no one told her it was cancer. When she found out through taking a sneak look at her chart on her doctor's desk, she was shocked to see that the prognosis said six to eighteen months to live. Her anger galvanized her. "Oh, no!" she said out loud. "I'm not going to have this. I'm going to get on with my life."

She continued her treatment, which included eight more operations but, at the same time, she returned to school. She decided to become a radiology technologist and after training moved to San Diego to work in a hospital.

Not liking the nine-to-five routine and still requiring far more than the normal number of sick days, she quit her job but started to fill in whenever different radiology departments needed extra help. The demand became so great that she asked friends to pitch in. Thus the seeds of a business were born.

Today Janis is the director of the company she founded: Radiology Relief, Inc. She has twenty to fifty part-time employees and grosses over $1 million per year. Her philosophy is simple: "Life's too short; I want to be free to enjoy it."

A year from now you may wish you had started today.

Karen Lamb

Herb Kelleher, head of Southwest Airlines, runs the most consistently profitable airline in the United States. With a sense of humor that is not merely contagious but virulent, Kelleher is surely the most outrageous CEO alive today. He runs his company with consummate people skills, a nose for cutting costs, and a consistent focus on fun. Kelleher has appeared at corporate headquarters dressed as Elvis, and on his planes he has dolled up as the Easter Bunny. When Southwest was named the official airline for Sea World, Kelleher showed his gratitude by painting a plane to look like Shamu, Sea World's killer whale.

Kelleher's attitude is reflected in Southwest's employees. His flight attendants have been known to organize trivia contests and seated relay races among passengers, deliver instructions in rap, hide in overhead baggage compartments, and give out prizes to fliers with the largest holes in their socks. "What we are looking for, first and foremost," he explains, "is a sense of humor. We hire attitudes."

Does this atmosphere of fun and camaraderie get in the way of efficiency, productivity, or profits? No, just the opposite. Kelleher and Southwest have demonstrated over and over that a sense of humor, combined with a desire to contribute, makes for a corporate culture that consistently promotes excellence. As a result, Southwest employees are by far the most productive and the most loyal in the industry. Meanwhile, Southwest has grown larger and more profitable year after year. And *Fortune* magazine recently referred to Kelleher as "America's best CEO."

It ain't braggin' if you can do it.

Dizzy Dean

The
Eagle's
Secret

Many obstacles run through each day. It is important to recognize them and prepare a plan of action because you can almost bet they will be there for you tomorrow. A breakthrough of any obstacle is success. I believe life is like a parade. A parade takes two kinds of people: the marchers and the watchers. The choice is mine! I want to be a marcher. I need a beginning and an end. I need help along the tough spots. I know I will only get this day once so I want it to be mine.

Elaine D'Agostino – Senior Executive Secretary, Becton Dickinson and Company

What do Norm, Janis, Herb, and Elaine have in common? They are all, of course, "thrivers." Thrivers know that life, with all of its absurdities and challenges, is ultimately the only parade in town and under no circumstances do they intend to be watchers. They want to march with all of the energy and commitment that they can muster. If life is a parade thrivers are going to participate fully.

Kenichi Ohmae, a Japanese management consultant, is the author of over sixty books, a contributor to the *Harvard Business Review* and the *Washington Post*, a much-in-demand speaker, and now wealthy enough to retire. He instead entered politics running for the office of governor of Tokyo. His purpose was not power but to fulfill the vision printed on his business card: **Let's make a good country.**

The electorate, however, was not ready for Ohmae's vision, and he placed fourth out of the six candidates. Asked why he would consider dirtying his impeccable reputation with politics, he replied: "I don't want to get to the end of my life and say 'Gee, I wish I had done that.'"

Thrivers are different, but what is their secret? Why do they continue to grow and prosper?

Simply put, thrivers are fully engaged in living. They exemplify, express, manifest, and model the attitudes and behaviors we have discussed throughout this book. Thrivers have a deep desire, whether life is a dress rehearsal or not, to be involved, to discover, to learn, to expand, to achieve, to enjoy, to laugh, to love, and to contribute. They may finish the parade spent and exhausted, but a fully lived life leaves you that way.

The eagle stood proudly on the edge of his nest. As he gazed at the mountains and valleys before him, the eagle's thoughts returned to his childhood. He could remember clearly his first attempts at flight. Time and time again he had fallen out of control toward the rocks below. Time and time again his ever vigilant mother was there to save him.

The eagle recalled asking her, "What's wrong? Am I not as powerful as you have led me to believe?" His mother's answer would provide for him one of the most extraordinary moments of his life. Sensing that he was at last ready, she had revealed the eagle's secret.

"All eagles were born to soar. It is why we were created. Our power, however, comes not from what we can see, it is in the unseen. It is the wind, not our wings, that lifts us to the high places. It is our vision, not our eyes, that makes us rulers of the skies. But, above all these, it is our spirit, not our speed, that leads us to be strong and free."